Conversational
ITALIAN

IN 7
DAYS

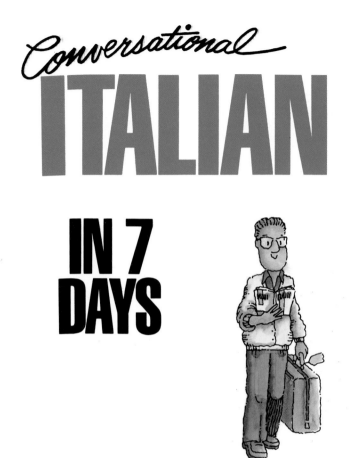

SHIRLEY BALDWIN & SARAH BOAS

D0166766

PASSPORT BOOKS
NTC/Contemporary Publishing Company

ACKNOWLEDGEMENTS

The authors and publishers are grateful to the following for supplying photographs or illustrations:

Adams Picture Library; J. Allan Cash Ltd; B. Furst; Vincent Martinelli; Spectrum Colour Library; Tony Stone Worldwide.

Library of Congress Cataloging-in-Publication Data
is available from the United States Library of Congress.

Published by Passport Books
An imprint of NTC/Contemporary Publishing Company
4255 West Touhy Avenue, Lincolnwood (Chicago), Illinois 60646-1975 U.S.A.
Copyright © 1991 by NTC/Contemporary Publishing Company
All rights reserved. No part of this book may be reproduced, stored in a retrieval
system, or transmitted in any form or by any means, electronic, mechanical,
photocopying, recording, or otherwise, without the prior permission of
NTC/Contemporary Publishing Company.
Printed in Hong Kong
International Standard Book Number: 0-8442-4498-8

8 9 0 WKT 9

CONTENTS

INTRODUCTION

Conversational Italian in 7 Days is a short course in Italian which will equip you to deal with everyday situations when you visit Italy: shopping, eating out, asking for directions, changing money, using the telephone, and so on.

The course is divided into 7 units, each corresponding to a day in the life of Marisa Cole (English teacher) and Paul Henderson (fashion buyer) during their week in Italy. Each unit begins with a dialogue, which introduces the essential language items in context. Key phrases are highlighted in the dialogues, and the phrasebook section which follows lists these and other useful phrases and tells you what they are in English.

Within these units, there are also short information sections in English on the topics covered, sections giving basic grammatical explanations, and a number of follow-up activities designed to be useful as well as fun. Answers can be checked in a key at the back of the book. English–Italian vocabulary is listed under topic headings on pp. 78–82, followed by an Italian–English vocabulary list. Also available with this program are 2 cassettes to help you practice your Italian.

Pronunciation

1   Each part of every word is sounded. Consonants are mostly similar to English ones, but vowels are "purer."

2   One part of every word is stressed more than the others. Usually this is the syllable before the last: c**o**me, andi**a**mo. Some words, however, are stressed on the last vowel, and when this happens the vowel always carries a written accent: caff**è**, cos**ì**. A few words have an irregular stress, and these just have to be learned as you go along: c**o**stano, des**i**dera, s**u**bito.

Vowels:

a (i) like *a* in *father:* b**a**nca

e (i) like *ai* in *chain:* p**e**ra
   (ii) like *e* in *peck:* **e**cco

i like *i* in *machine:* vic**i**no

o (i) like *o* in *sole:* s**o**no
   (ii) like *o* in *not:* n**o**tte

u like *oo* in *moon:* **u**na

Consonants: *similar to English but with the following exceptions:*

c	(i) before **e, i** like *ch* in *chin:*	centro	**h**	never pronounced	
			r	or **rr**, always rolled:	sera
	(ii) elsewhere like *c* in *cat:*	comprare	**s**	(i) like *s* in *sun:*	questa
ch	like *k* in *key:*	chiamo		(ii) like *z* in *zoo:*	esatto
g	(i) before **e, i** like *j* in *jam:*	giorno	**sc**	(i) before **e, i** like *sh* in *shin:*	pesce
	(ii) elsewhere like *g* in *got:*	prego		(ii) elsewhere like *sk* in *skin:*	pescare
gh	like *g* in *got:*	traghetto	**z**	(i) like *ts* in *rats:*	grazie
gl	like *ll* in *million:*	biglietto		(ii) like *ds* in *beds:*	mezzo
gn	like *ni* in *onion:*	bagno			

GREETINGS AND INTRODUCTIONS

When arriving in Italy, you will find customs and passport procedures standard and easy to follow, because much information is given in English as well as Italian. You should check your duty-free allowances before setting out on your journey. Look out for these signs: **DOGANA** (Customs) and **CONTROLLO PASSAPORTI** (Passport Control).

come si chiama?/what's your name?

Paul Henderson (38), a fashion buyer, is on a trip to Florence to buy clothes and accessories for his clothing store. He arrives at Pisa airport, where he has arranged to be met by Raffaella Festoso (32), a designer for an Italian fashion house.

Raffaella: **Buongiorno. Come si chiama, per favore?**
Paul: **Io sono** Paul Henderson. **E lei, come si chiama**, signora?
Raffaella: **Mi chiamo** Raffaella Festoso. **Piacere.**
Paul: **Molto lieto**, signora.
Raffaella: La mia macchina è qui vicino. Andiamo a Firenze?
Paul: Benissimo, andiamo.

1

Arriving on the same plane is Marisa Cole (22), a teacher who has come to Italy to see her boyfriend Giancarlo (27) and to apply for a teaching job. It is Giancarlo's father, Enrico, and mother, Anna, who come to meet her.

Anna:	**Buongiorno, scusi, lei è la signorina Cole?**
Marisa:	Sì, sono Marisa Cole. Lei è la signora Lazzarini?
Anna:	Sì, sono la madre di Giancarlo. **Le presento mio marito,** Enrico.
Enrico:	Ben arrivata, signorina! Ha fatto buon viaggio?
Marisa:	Sì, ottimo, grazie.
Anna:	Marisa, dov'è il suo bagaglio?
Marisa:	È proprio qui.
Anna:	Enrico, **per piacere,** prendi la valigia e andiamo a casa.

(Enrico picks up Marisa's case)

Marisa:	**Grazie.**
Enrico:	**Prego,** signorina. Andiamo. È ora di pranzo.

Saying hello and goodbye Note that **Buongiorno, Buonasera,** and **Ciao** can be used when saying *Hello* or *Goodbye*. With friends, relatives, or children, you can use **Ciao.**

buongiorno	hello/good morning/good afternoon
buonasera	hello/good afternoon/good evening
buonanotte	good night
arrivederci	goodbye (informal)
arrivederla	goodbye (formal)

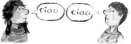

Ciao, Giulia.	Hello, Julia.	
Ciao, Marco.	Bye, Mark.	

You should address a man as **signore,** a woman as **signora,** and a girl or young unmarried woman as **signorina.** These titles are used much more frequently on their own than, for example, *sir* or *madam* are in English.

Buongiorno, signore.*	Good morning. (to a man)
Buonasera, signora.	Good evening. (to a woman)
Buonanotte, signorina.	Good night. (to a young woman or girl)

***Signore** becomes **signor** in front of a name: **il signor Bianchini.** When addressing a man and a woman together, you say **signori.**

Greetings and introductions

(Lei) è il signor . . . ?	Are you Mr. . . . ?
(Io) sono . . .	I am . . .
Come si chiama?	What's your name? (formal)/What's his/her name?

Come ti chiami?	What's your name? (familiar)
Mi chiamo . . .	My name is . . .
Piacere (di conoscerla).	Pleased to meet you.
Piacere/molto piacere/molto lieto.	Nice to meet you.
Piacere mio.	My pleasure.
Le presento mia moglie/mio marito.	This is my wife/my husband.
Ben arrivato! Ben arrivata!	Welcome!

Words of courtesy

per favore/per piacere	please
Grazie.	Thank you.
Grazie tante/grazie mille.	Thank you very much.
Prego.	You're welcome.
Non c'è di che.	Don't mention it.
Scusi.	Excuse me.
Molto gentile.	It's very kind of you.

Yes and no

sì/no	yes/no	**Sì, grazie/No**	Yes, please/No,
Non è . . .	It's not . . .	**grazie.**	thank you.

USEFUL WORDS AND PHRASES (Dialogue 1)

la mia macchina	my car	**benissimo**	fine, excellent
è qui vicino	is quite near	**Andiamo a Firenze.**	Let's go to Florence.

USEFUL WORDS AND PHRASES (Dialogue 2)

il padre di/la madre di	the father of/the mother of
Ha fatto buon viaggio?	Have you had a good trip?
Ottimo!	Great!
Dov'è . . . ?	Where is . . . ?
il suo bagaglio	your luggage
È proprio qui.	It's right here.
Prendi la sua valigia.	Take her case.
Andiamo a casa.	Let's go home.

Enrico
il padre

Anna
la madre

Giancarlo
il figlio

Margherita
la figlia

3

the way it works

People and things

In Italian, words for people and things are either masculine or feminine. The word for *the* is normally **il** for a masculine noun—**il passaporto** passport—and **la** for a feminine noun—**la valigia** suitcase.

When a noun begins with a vowel, however, you use **l'** (**l'albergo** hotel), and with a masculine noun that begins with **z** or **s + consonant** you use **lo** (**lo zucchero** sugar). Most nouns ending in -**o** are masculine, and most nouns ending in -**a** are feminine. To make a noun plural, -**o** changes to -**i** and -**a** changes to -**e**. The word for "the" also changes:

	singular	plural		singular	plural
masc.	il passaporto	i passaporti	*fem.*	la valigia	le valigie

Some nouns end in -**e** in the singular. Some of these are masculine (**il padre, il piacere**) and others are feminine (**la madre, la notte** night). All these nouns change the -**e** to -**i** in the plural: **i padri, le madri, le notti**.

I am, you are

Io sono Paul Henderson.	I am Paul Henderson.
Lei è il signor Henderson.	You are Mr. Henderson.

The most commonly used verb in Italian for "to be" is **essere**.

(io) sono	I am	(noi) siamo	we are
(tu) sei	you are (familiar)	(voi) siete	you are
(lei) è	you are (formal), she is		
(lui) è	he is	(loro) sono	they are

The words **io** (I), **tu** (you), **lei** (you, she), etc., are subject pronouns. They are not normally needed because the form and ending of the verb itself indicate who is the subject of the verb. They are, however, used when confusion might otherwise arise, or for emphasis.

Note that there are two words for "you" in Italian. With people you don't know well, it is probably safer to use the formal **lei** form. With everyone else (particularly with friends and relations), you can use **tu**, which is becoming much more widely used.

The **tu** form takes the second person of the verb, while the **lei** form takes the third person, just like *he/she*.

Asking questions

There are various ways in which you can ask a question in Italian. For questions to which the answer is *Yes* or *No*, you can use the same word order as a statement but with a questioning tone of voice.

Lei è il signor Henderson?	Are you Mr. Henderson?
Lei è la signora Lazzarini?	Are you Mrs. Lazzarini?

If you are almost sure the answer is *Yes*, you sometimes add **Vero?** or **No?** (aren't you?/Isn't it? etc.).

Other kinds of question start with words such as *Who?, What?* or *Where?*

Dov'è* il suo bagaglio?	Where is your luggage?

*Note that **Dove** is shortened to **Dov'** before **è**.

Saying no

To make a negative statement, just add **non** before the verb.
No, **non** sono il signor Henderson.   No, I'm not Mr. Henderson.

My, your, his/her (singular)

Possessive adjectives usually come before the noun and are preceded by **il** or **la**.
la mia macchina (my car)   **il suo** bagaglio (your luggage)
The endings vary according to whether the thing or person possessed is masculine
or feminine, singular or plural:

il mio bagaglio	my luggage	**la mia** valigia	my suitcase
il tuo bagaglio	your luggage	**la tua** valigia	your suitcase (fam)
il suo bagaglio	your luggage/his/ her luggage	**la sua** valigia	your suitcase (formal)/his/her suitcase

things to do

1.1 Buongiorno, signora. Raffaella is meeting a lot of people today! How
does she greet them all? Add **signore**, **signora**, or **signorina** when
appropriate:

In the morning:
  1 Mr. Rinaldi (an elderly business colleague)
  2 Mrs. Marzella (a shopkeeper)
  3 Claudia (her cousin)

In the afternoon:
  4 Mr. and Mrs. Fallaci
  5 Miss Giulia Neri (a friend of her mother)
  6 Mauro (a friend from work)

1.2 Come si chiama? Practice the following mini-conversations:
  1 Customs officer to Mr. Jones:
    Customs officer: Come si chiama?
    Henry Jones: . . .
    He turns to Mrs. Jones:
    Customs officer: Lei è la signora Jones?
    Susan Jones   Sì, . . .
  2 Radio interviewer talks to Patricia Fox and her young son, Ben:
    Interviewer: Scusi, come si chiama, per favore?
    Patricia: . . .
    Interviewer: E suo figlio, come si chiama?
    Patricia: . . .

1.3 Can you match the following questions and answers:
  1 Come si chiama, per favore?   (a) Sì, sono la signora Bruni.
  2 Lei è la signora Bruni?   (b) No, non sono il padre di Franco.
  3 Dov'è il suo bagaglio?   (c) Mi chiamo Maria Roberti.
  4 È la sua valigia?   (d) È proprio qui.
  5 Lei è il padre di Franco?   (e) No, non è la mia.

RESERVING A HOTEL ROOM

Accommodation Hotels **(alberghi)** are classified into five categories ranging from the De Luxe **(Categoria Lusso)** to the modest Class IV. Detailed lists of hotels, etc., can be obtained from the Italian National Tourist Office (ENIT) or from the local **Azienda di Turismo** (Tourist Office). Reservations are desirable, particularly in tourist areas and during the high season.

Other forms of accommodation include boarding houses **(pensioni** or **locande)**, farmhouses, mountain huts **(rifugi alpini)**, villas, and apartments **(appartamenti)**, details of which can also be obtained from ENIT. There are also about 50 youth hostels **(alberghi per la gioventù)** for members of youth hostel associations.

When you arrive, you may have to fill out a registration form **(una scheda)** giving details of nationality, address, occupation, passport number, etc. Service **(il servizio)** and VAT **(TVA)**, or Value-Added Tax, is usually included in the charge for the room, but breakfast is often not included. When paying the bill **(il conto)**, remember that you should obtain an official receipt for it.

all'albergo/at the hotel

Raffaella takes Paul to his hotel to check in before going on to her office.

Direttore: Buonasera, signori, desiderano?
Paul: **Ho prenotato una camera.**
Direttore: Sì. Il suo nome, per favore.
Paul: Henderson.
Direttore: Bene. Un attimo, per favore. (checks his list) Henderson . . . Ah sì. **Camera singola con bagno, per tre notti.** Ecco la chiave, signore. Posso avere il suo passaporto, per favore?
Paul: Sì, certo. (hands it over)
Direttore: Grazie. (calls the porter) Mario, porta le valigie del signore al primo piano, camera numero quindici.
Paul: **A che ora è la prima colazione?**
Direttore: Dalle sette alle nove e mezzo.

ha una camera?/do you have a room?

Raffaella wants a room for herself and her husband, Pietro.

Raffaella: **Anch'io vorrei prenotare una camera.** Ha una doppia, per favore?
Direttore: Sì signora. Con bagno o con doccia?
Raffaella: **Con bagno.**
Direttore: Per quanto?
Raffaella: **Soltanto per una notte.**
Direttore: Sì, ce l'abbiamo, . . . ma solo con doccia.
Raffaella: **Va bene** con doccia. **Qual'è il prezzo** della camera?
Direttore: Novantamila lire per notte.
Raffaella: **È compresa** la colazione?
Direttore: No, la colazione è a parte. Sono quattromila lire in più.
Raffaella: Bè . . . è un po' cara ma . . . Va bene, **la prendo.**

USEFUL WORDS AND PHRASES

un attimo	one moment
sì, certo	yes, of course
Torno domani mattina.	I'll come back tomorrow morning.
A domani!	Till tomorrow!
Va bene.	OK.
benissimo	fine, excellent
Bè . . .	Well . . .

Reserving a hotel room

il direttore	manager
Desiderano?	Can I help you? What do you want?
Ha una camera?	Do you have a room?
Avete camere libere?	Do you have any vacancies?
Ho prenotato una camera.	I have reserved a room.
Ho una prenotazione.	I have a reservation.
Il suo nome, per favore?	Your name, please?
Vorrei prenotare una camera	I'd like to reserve a room
per sabato	for Saturday
. . . doppia/singola	. . . double/single
. . . con letto matrimoniale	. . . with a double bed
. . . con due letti	. . . with two beds
. . . con bagno/con doccia	. . . with bath/with shower
. . . senza bagno/solo con doccia	. . . without bath/with just a shower
. . . con balcone/con vista sul mare	. . . with a balcony/with a view of the sea
. . . sul davanti/. . . sul retro	. . . at the front/at the back
l'aria condizionata	air conditioning
il riscaldamento	heating
l'acqua calda/il gabinetto	hot water/toilet
Per quanto?	For how long?
per una settimana/tre notti	for a week/three nights
soltanto per una notte	one night only
Sì, ce l'abbiamo.	We have one.
L'albergo è completo.	The hotel is full.

(For numbers, see list on p. 78)

Spett. La Direzione
    Hotel Lungano

Desidero passare una settimana in Firenze e vorrei sapere se
avete disponibile una camera singola con bagno da 22
Settembre. In caso affermativo Vi prego di comunicarmi
il prezzo per la camera e colazione.
    In attesa di Vostra conferma porgo
Cordiali saluti
        Lesmy Robertson

Checking the price and what it includes

Qual è il prezzo della camera?	What's the price of the room?
per la pensione completa	for full board
per mezza pensione	for half board
novatamila lire per notte	90,000 lira per night
la colazione	breakfast
il servizio	service
È compresa la colazione?	Is breakfast included?
prima colazione compresa	breakfast included
tutto compreso	everything included

La colazione è a parte.	Breakfast is not included.
in più	over and above
A che ora è la colazione?	What time is breakfast?
dalle sette alle nove e mezzo	from 7 to 9:30 a.m.
Posso vedere la camera?	Can I see the room?
È un po' (troppo) cara.	It's too expensive.
Non ha nulla di meno caro?	Don't you have anything cheaper?
Va bene, la prendo.	That's fine, I'll take it.

Keys, documents, and luggage

Qual è il numero della mia camera?	What's the number of my room?
camera numero quindici	room number 15
Ecco la chiave.	Here is the key.
Per favore la chiave.	The key, please.
Posso avere il suo passaporto?	Please could I have your passport?
i documenti	the documents
la carta d'identità	identity card
Può compilare questa scheda?	Can you fill out this form?
il facchino	porter
Può far portare su i nostri bagagli?	Can you have our luggage sent up?
Porta le valigie	Carry the suitcases
al primo piano/al secondo piano.	to the first floor/second floor.
Avete garage?	Do you have a garage?
Dove posso parcheggiare?	Where can I park?

The bill

Partirò domani mattina.	I'm leaving tomorrow morning.
Mi faccia il conto, per favore.	Could I have the bill please?
Ha fatto un errore nel conto, credo.	I think there is a mistake in the bill.
Accettate le carte di credito?	Do you accept credit cards?
Tutto è compreso?	Is everything included?

ORDERING DRINKS

Italian bars As well as alcoholic beverages, bars and cafés serve coffee, soft drinks, and snacks. You sometimes have to pay for your drink beforehand to a cashier. After paying, you take your receipt (**lo scontrino**) to the counter and tell the person at the bar what you want. You can then stand at the bar to have your drink. If you want to sit at a table (**un tavolo**) and be served by a waiter (**un cameriere**), you pay afterwards and this is sometimes more expensive.

9

che cosa prendi?/what'll you have?

Before supper, Anna and Enrico take Marisa to a **caffè** where Giancarlo joins them.

Giancarlo:	**Ciao, Marisa, come stai?**
Marisa:	**Bene, grazie, e tu?**
Giancarlo:	**Così, così.** Hai fatto buon viaggio?
Marisa:	Sì, grazie.

(The waiter comes to take their order)

Giancarlo:	Cosa prendi?
Marisa:	**Un martini con ghiaccio per me.**
Giancarlo:	(turns to his parents) E per voi, mamma e papà?
Anna:	Per me un bicchiere di vino bianco.
Enrico:	**Io prendo una birra, grazie.**
Giancarlo:	(to waiter) Per la signorina un martini con ghiaccio, per la signora un bicchiere di vino bianco e per il signore una birra. E per me . . . un bitter, per favore.
Cameriere:	Benissimo, signori.

(He brings the drinks)

Giancarlo:	Grazie. Allora, **facciamo un brindisi! Cin-cin!**

Here is a list of the drinks mentioned in the dialogue plus a few more . . .

un **caffè** (espresso)	strong black coffee	una **spremuta d'arancia**	fresh orange juice
un **cappuccino**	coffee with frothy milk	di **limone**	fresh lemon juice
un **caffelatte**	coffee with ordinary milk	un'**acqua minerale**	mineral water
un **caffè macchiato**	with a dash of milk	un **bicchiere di**	a glass of
		vino rosso	red wine
un **tè freddo**	iced tea	**vino bianco**	white wine
un **tè al latte**	tea with milk	una **birra (nazionale)**	beer from Italy
un **tè al limone**	tea with lemon	un **aperitivo della casa**	house aperitif
		una **birra (estera)**	foreign beer
una **coca-cola**	coke	un **martini**	martini
un'**aranciata**	orangeade	un **vermut**	vermouth
una **limonata**	lemonade	un **bitter**	type of aperitif
un **succo di frutta**	fruit juice	un **americano**	type of aperitif
di **mela**	apple juice	un **frullato**	milkshake

Ordering drinks

Cosa prendi?/Cosa prende?	What'll you have?
(Cosa) desiderano?	What would you like?
un martini con ghiaccio	a martini with ice
per me/per voi	for me/for you (plural)

un bicchiere di . . .	a glass of . . .
Io prendo . . .	I'll have . . .
Mi dà . . .	Give me . . .
Ecco lo scontrino.	Here's the receipt.
Facciamo un brindisi!	Let's make a toast!
Cin-cin!	Cheers!

the way it works

Un/Una

un albergo	a hotel	una camera	a room
un martini	a martini	una birra	a beer

The usual word for "a" or "an" in Italian is **un** for masculine nouns and **una** for feminine nouns.

However, with masculine words which begin with **s** + a second consonant, or with **z** or **ps**, you say **uno**: **uno scontrino** a receipt, **uno zucchino** a zucchini.

With feminine words which begin with a vowel, you use **un'**: **un'aranciata** an orangeade.

Asking how someone is

To ask how some is, say:	**Come sta?** (formal) or **Come stai?** (familiar)
Answers might include:	**Sto bene, grazie, e lei?** (formal) or **Bene, grazie, e tu?** (familiar)
To which the first person might reply:	**Bene, grazie.**
Other phrases about one's state of health include:	**Così, così.** So, so.
	Non c'è male. Not too bad.
	Benissimo! Fine!

Note that **sto, stai, sta** are parts of the verb **stare** "to be," which is mainly used to ask and describe how one feels.

Asking and telling the time (There is a list of numbers on p. 78)

To ask the time you say: **Che ora è?** *or* **Che ore sono?**

To tell the time, you say:

È l'una	(It's one o'clock)
È mezzogiorno	(It's noon)
Sono le tre	(It's three o'clock, etc.)

meno quarto   e quarto

e mezzo

To say at what time something happens:

La colazione è alle otto.	Breakfast is at 8 o'clock.
. . . è dalle sette alle nove e mezzo	. . . from 7 till 9:30

11

Asking if something you want is available

Look at the following phrases:

Ha/Avete una camera?	Do you have a room?
Sì, ce l'**abbiamo**.	We have one.

These are parts of the useful verb **avere** (to have):

ho	I have	**abbiamo**	we have
hai	you have (familiar)	**avete**	you have
ha	you have (formal)		
ha	he/she/it has	**hanno**	they have

things to do

1.4 **Vorrei una camera**. You are a travel agent making a hotel reservation for a party of people, all of whom have different requirements . . .

  1 one double room with bath   **4** one single room with a sea view

  2 one single room with shower   **5** two single rooms with bath

  3 one double room with twin beds

1.5 **Che ore sono?** A passerby asks you the time. But unfortunately each member of your family has a different time . . .

  Sone le . . .

Someone's watch is rather slow   and someone's watch must have stopped altogether!

1.6 **Desidera?** You have paid the cashier and received your **scontrino**. You are about to present it to the **barista** (bartender). This is what you want and you give him your order:

  Mi dà . . .

FINDING YOUR WAY AROUND

Breakfast (**la colazione**) is not considered a very important meal in Italy, and most people just have coffee (**caffelatte** is a mild black coffee with hot milk) or fruit juice and bread and butter.

dov'è il duomo?/where is the cathedral?

Paul doesn't know Florence, and he is eager to see the sights; so at breakfast in the hotel, he asks Raffaella for details.

Paul: **Dov'è il Duomo, per favore?**
Raffaella: È in centro. Passi per il Ponte Vecchio e vada sempre dritto.
Paul: **È lontano da qui?**
Raffaella: No, da qui è dieci minuti a piedi.
Paul: E dov'è la Galleria degli Uffizi?
Raffaella: Dopo il Ponte giri a destra. È proprio vicino.
Paul: **Vorrei vedere** anche il Palazzo Vecchio.
Raffaella: Ah sì, è vicino alla Galleria degli Uffizi, in Piazza della Signoria.
Paul: **E c'è una tabaccheria qui vicino?**
Raffaella: Sì . . ., ce n'è una en Via dei Velluti. Prenda la prima a sinistra poi la seconda a destra. È sulla destra a cento metri.

The waiter comes over to take their order.

Cameriere: Prego, signori?
Raffaella: Io prendo un espresso. Cosa prende, Paul?
Paul: Per me, un caffelatte e un panino.
Cameriere: Subito, signori.

Finding your way

Dov'è il Duomo?	Where is the cathedral?
È in centro.	It's in the center of town.
Passi per . . .	Go along/across . . .
il Ponte Vecchio	The Old Bridge

Italian	English
Vada sempre dritto.	Go straight ahead.
È lontano da qui?	Is it far from here?
abbastanza lontano	quite a long way
è dieci minuti a piedi	ten minutes on foot
La Galleria degli Uffizi	The Uffizi Gallery
dopo il ponte	after the bridge
Giri a destra.	Turn right.
È proprio vicino.	It's very near.
Vorrei vedere anche . . .	I'd also like to see . . .
Il Palazzo Vecchio	The Old Palace
vicino a . . .	near (to) . . .
Piazza della Signoria	Signoria Square
C'è una tabaccheria qui vicino?	Is there a tobacco shop near here?
Ce n'è una in Via dei Velluti.	There's one in Via dei Velluti.
Prenda la prima a sinistra.	Take the first on the left.
la seconda a destra	the second on the right
sulla destra/sulla sinistra	on the right/on the left
a due passi	two steps (very near)

di dov'è?/where are you from?

Marisa is looking for a teaching job in Italy, and has an appointment at a language school. While waiting to see the director, she talks to one of the other teachers.

Marco: Buongiorno. **È americana?**

Marisa: No, **sono inglese.** E lei, **di dov'è?**

Marco: Sono italiano, **di Vicenza.** Di dov'è in Inghilterra?

Marisa: **Sono di Londra.**

Marco: **Ah! Mi piace tanto Londra. Ma parla l'italiano molto bene.**

Marisa: Grazie. Mia nonna è italiana. Abita a Napoli. Senta, vorrei parlare con il direttore.

Marco: Ha un appuntamento?

Marisa: Sì, alle dieci e mezzo.

(At that moment the director comes in)

Direttore: Ah, buongiorno, s'accomodi, signorina. È americana?

la lingua inglese s'impara al **BRITISH SCHOOL**

LIVORNO Via Santo, 62 · FIRENZE Via dei Servi, 7

PISA Via Righetti, 33 — PISTOIA Galleria Nazionale, 21

Nationalities and languages

Italian	English
È americano?/americana?	Are you American? (male/female)
Sono inglese.	I am English.
Sono canadese/irlandese.	I'm Canadian/Irish.
Sono italiano/italiana.	I am Italian. (male/female)
Mia nonna è italiana.	My grandmother is Italian.
di Vicenza/di Nuova York	from Vicenza/New York
Abita a Napoli.	She lives in Naples.
Parla l'italiano.	You speak Italian.
Parla l'italiano?/l'inglese?	Do you speak Italian?/English?
Parlo tedesco/francese.	I speak German/French.
Capisce l'inglese?	Do you understand English?

Capisco/Non capisco.	I understand/don't understand.
Capisco ma non parlo.	I understand but I don't speak.
più lentamente	more slowly
Ho capito.	I understand.

USEFUL WORDS AND PHRASES

Senta!	Listen!
Vorrei parlare con . . .	I'd like to speak to . . .
Ha un appuntamento?	Do you have an appointment?
S'accomodi.	Sit down, make yourself comfortable.

the way it works

Asking for and understanding directions

The easiest way of doing this is to say: **Dov'è . . . ?**

Dov'e il duomo?   Where is the cathedral?

You will probably hear some of the following instructions:

| **vada** . . . | go . . . | **passi per** . . . | go along . . . |
| **prenda** . . . | take . . . | **giri** . . . | turn . . . |

Listen in particular for the following phrases in reply:

a destra   right

sempre dritto   straight ahead

a sinistra   left

More specifically:

la prima a destra   first street on the right

la seconda a sinistra   second street on the left

And sometimes you will be told how far it is
and how long it will take you:

È a due chilometri. It's two kilometers away.

È a cinque minuti. It's five minutes away.

There is/there are

In Italian you say simply: **C'è** (there is) or **Ci sono** (there are).

| **C'è una banca.** | There is a bank. |
| **Ci sono tre camere.** | There are three rooms. |

To say "there is one (of them)" you insert **ne**:

| **Ce n'è uno/Ce n'è una.** | There is one. (masc/fem) |

Note that the question form is identical:

| **C'è una banca?** | Is there a bank? |

Some useful place words

accanto a	beside	in fondo	at/to the end
dopo	after	lì, qui	there, here
dietro	behind	fino a	as far as, until
davanti	in front	l'incrocio	corner
di fronte	opposite	il semaforo	traffic lights
per	along	il ponte	bridge

15

At/to/from/of/in/on

There are several examples of these useful words in this unit.

a Napoli	at Naples	**a** destra	(to the) right
di Londra	from London	**da** qui	from here
in Piazza Santa Croce	in Santa Croce Square		

When used with the definite article (at the, from the, of the, etc.), these words combine with **il, lo, la, l', i, gli, le**:

alla galleria **degli** Uffizi	to the Gallery of the Uffizi
La Piazza **della** Repubblica	the Square of the Republic
sulla destra	on the right-hand side

Here is a table giving all the combined forms:

		il	lo	la	l'	i	gli	le
to/at	a	al	allo	alla	all'	ai	agli	alle
by/from	da	dal	dallo	dalla	dall'	dai	dagli	dalle
of/from	di	del	dello	della	dell'	dei	degli	delle
in/into	in	nel	nello	nella	nell'	nei	negli	nelle
on	su	sul	sullo	sulla	sull'	sui	sugli	sulle

Note that **in** is used in several colloquial expressions without the definite article, to mean "to" or "in":

Vado **in** albergo/**in** banca.   I'm going to the hotel/to the bank.

I'd like to . . .

Note the very useful expression **vorrei**, which is used to mean "I'd like . . ." and is followed by an infinitive (or dictionary form):

Vorrei vedere . . .   I'd like to see   **Vorrei parlare** . . .   I'd like to speak

Vorrei is part of the verb **volere** (to want). Here is the present tense:

voglio	I want	**vogliamo**	we want
vuoi	you want (familiar)	**volete**	you want
vuole	he/she wants, you want	**vogliono**	they want, you want

Saying where you come from

If someone asks you:	**Di dov'è (lei)?**
you will be able to answer:	**Sono di Chicago, etc.**
You might be asked:	**È irlandese?**
to which you can reply:	**Sì, sono irlandese** *or*
	No, sono americano.

Regular verbs group 1 (parlare)

Parlare is an example of an **-are** verb (named after its infinitive—or dictionary—ending), which is the first of four regular verb groups in Italian.

Parla l'inglese?	Do you speak English?
Parla l'italiano molto bene.	You speak Italian very well.

It is worth noting how the verb **parlare** (to speak) is formed:

parl**o**	I speak	parl**iamo**	we speak
parl**i**	you speak (familiar)	parl**ate**	you speak
parl**a**	he/she speaks, you speak (formal)	parl**ano**	they speak, you speak (formal)

things to do

2.1 You want to visit the following places, but you are not sure where they are. How do you ask?

1 la Piazza della Repubblica
2 il Palazzo Veccio

3 la Galleria degli Uffizi
4 l'Azienda di Turismo
5 La posta

2.2 Look at the map of Florence (Firenze). You are standing (marked **X**) on the Via del Corso at the corner of the Via dei Calzaioli (the street of the shoemakers). Can you tell from the following instructions which of the places above you are being directed to?

1 Giri a sinistra e vada sempre dritto alla Piazza della Signoria. È sulla sinistra, in fondo alla piazza.
2 Giri a sinistra e prenda la seconda a destra. Vada fino al primo incrocio. È lì di fronte.
3 Vada dritto fino al secondo incrocio.
4 Passi per la Piazza della Repubblica e vada sempre dritto. In Via dei Tornabuoni giri a destra. È sulla sinistra.

2.3 Can you match the following questions and answers?

1 Parla l'italiano?
2 Di dov'è?
3 C'è una toilette qui?
4 Dov'è il Palazzo?
5 Dove abita?

(a) A Londra.
(b) È in fondo alla piazza.
(c) Capisco ma non parlo.
(d) Di Chicago.
(e) Sì, lì sulla sinistra.

SHOPPING

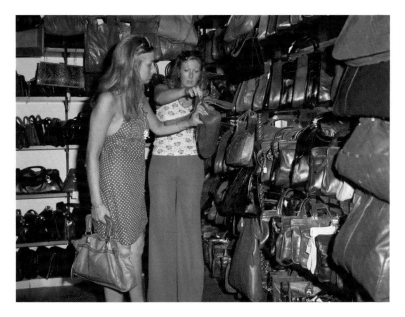

quanto costa?/how much is it?

Marisa decides to go and buy herself a handbag. She goes to a leather shop (**una pelletteria**) in the Piazza Santa Croce.

Commessa: Buongiorno, signorina. Desidera?

Marisa: **Vorrei** una borsa di pelle.

Commessa: Va bene. Che colore?

Marisa: Bè . . . nera o marrone.

Commessa: S'accomodi, signorina. (She goes to get a selection) Le piace questa nera?

Marisa: Sì **è bella ma è un po'grande.** (Sees one on a shelf behind the counter) Quella lì è più piccola, quella nera. **Mi fa vedere quella,** per favore?

Commessa: Sì certo. (She gets it down) Eccola.

Marisa: **È bellissima. Quanto costa?**

Commessa: Questa? Costa novantasettemila.

Marisa: **È un po'cara.** Ma è bella e spaziosa.

Commessa: È di ottima qualità, signorina.

Marisa: **Mi piace molto** . . . Sì, **la prendo.**

Shopping—buying a handbag

una borsa di pelle	leather handbag
Che colore?	What color?
nero/a, marrone	black, brown
Le piace . . . ?	Do you like . . . ?
È bello/a.	It's beautiful.
un po'(troppo) grande	a bit too big
troppo piccolo/a	too small
non mi piace	I don't like
questo/a, quello/a	this (one), that (one)
più piccolo/a, più grande	smaller/larger
Mi fa vedere . . . ?	Please could you show me . . . ?
bellissimo/a	very beautiful
Costa novantasettemila.	It costs 97,000 lira.
un po'caro/a	a bit expensive
spazioso/a	spacious
di ottima qualità	top quality
Mi piace molto.	I like it very much.
Lo/la prendo, li/le prendo	I'll have it, I'll have them.
Quanto costa?/Quanto costano?	How much does it/do they cost?
S'accomodi alla cassa.	Please go to the cashier.
Accettate carte di credito?	Do you accept credit cards?

mi piace molto/I like it very much

Paul arrives at the Trade Fair with Raffaella to meet the directors of various Italian fashion houses. He stops at Moda Italiana.

Paul: (to the secretary) Buongiorno. Sono Paul Henderson, direttore della ditta inglese "Fashion Link." Ho un appuntamento con il suo direttore alle 15.00. Ecco il mio biglietto da visita.

Segretaria: Sì, un momento. Prego, signore, s'accomodi.

(They start looking around)

Raffaella: Questo vestito bianco e nero è molto bello. Le piace, Paul?

Paul: Sì è bello, ma **preferisco quello** là. **Mi piacciono questi** pantaloni larghi e comodi.

Raffaella: Quella gonna a quadretti è molto stravagante!

Paul: **Non mi piace molto** quella giacca corta. È troppo stretta.

Raffaella: Ma guardi quel cappello giallo! Che colore!

Paul: D'accordo. Ah! Ecco il direttore.

(The director comes over to greet them)

Direttore: Buongiorno, signor Henderson. Le piacciono i miei modelli per l'estate?

19

Paul	Sì, certo. Per cominciare, può farmi un preventivo per questi vestiti bianchi di seta e per quelle gonne di cotone.
Direttore:	Benissimo! S'accomodi nel mio ufficio, signori.

Buying clothes

questo vestito bianco e nero	this black and white dress
molto bello	very pretty
preferisco	I prefer
quello lì	that one over there
questo qui	this one here
mi piacciono	I like (plural)
questi pantaloni	these pants
È/Sono troppo . . .	It is/They are too . . .
largo/larga/larghi/larghe	large, wide
lungo/lunga/lunghi/lunghe	long
comodo/a/i/e	comfortable
corto/a/i/e	short
stretto/a/i/e	narrow, tight
quella gonna	that skirt
a quadretti	checked, with checks
È molto stravagante.	It is very odd.
quella giacca	that jacket
Ma guardi quel cappello giallo!	But look at that yellow hat!
Di che colore?	What color?
Che colore!	What a color!
Non ha qualcosa . . . ?	Don't you have anything . . . ?
. . . migliore/meno caro	. . . better/cheaper
No, grazie, è tutto.	No thanks, that's all.

Sizes

Women's dresses

American	6	8	10	12	14	16	18
Italian	36	38	40	42	44	46	48

Women's shoes

American	6½	7	7½	8	8½	9	9½
Italian	36	37	38	38½	39	40	41

Collar sizes

American	14	14½	15	15½	16	16½	17
Italian	36	37	38	39–40	41	42	43

Che numero?	What size (shoes)?
Che taglia?	What size (clothes)?
taglia quarantadue	size 42
un piao di scarpe	a pair of shoes
Posso provarlo?	Can I try it on?
Come va?/Come vanno?	How does it/do they look?
Non va bene.	It doesn't fit.
Ha qualcosa . . . ?	Do you have anything . . . ?
. . . di più piccolo/grande	. . . bigger/smaller

(For colors and clothes items, see p. 79–80)

Other useful phrases

Ecco . . .	Here is . . .
il mio biglietto da visita	my business card
per cominciare	to start with
Può farmi un preventivo?	Can you give me an estimate?
di seta/di cotone	silk/cotton

the way it works

I like it!

You say: **Mi piace** for ''I like . . .'' (one thing) and **Mi piacciono** for ''I like . . .'' (more than one).

Mi piace questa camicia.	I like this shirt.
Mi piacciono questi maglioni.	I like these sweaters.
Le piace questa borsa?	Do you like this purse?

It's lovely!

Look at the following phrases from the dialogues:

Questo vestito è molto bello.	This dress is very nice.
(La borsa) è bella e spaziosa.	(The bag) is pretty and spacious.

The ending of the adjective changes according to the gender of the noun it accompanies. Adjectives which end in **-o** in the masculine change to **-a** in the feminine, and to **-i** or **-e** in the plural:

Le scarpe sono troppo strette.	The shoes are too tight.
I sandali sono molto comodi.	The sandals are very comfortable.

Note that **molto** (very) and **troppo** (too much) do *not* change:

	masc	fem		masc	fem
sing	bello	bella	*sing*	piccolo	piccola
plural	belli	belle	*plural*	piccoli	piccole

Adjectives which end in **-e** (masculine and feminine) change to **-i** in the plural:

sing	grande, inglese	*plural*	grandi, inglesi

Note: Adjectives usually follow the noun. However, some common adjectives such as **bello** can precede the noun, in which case the forms of the adjective endings are similar to those of the definite article: un **bel** vestito, una **bella** gonna, uno **bello** spezzato, un **bell'**abito.

This and that, these and those

Questo means ''this'' and ''this one,'' and **quello** means ''that'' and ''that one.'' Here are the endings for **questo**:

	this	*these*
masc	questo modello, quest'anello	questi modelli
fem	questa borsa	queste borse

Quello is more complicated, following the same rules as the definite article:

	that	*those*
masc	quel modello	quei modelli
	quello zoccolo *(clog)*	quegli zoccoli *(clogs)*
	quell'albergo	quegli alberghi
fem	quella borsa	quelle borse
	quell'arancia	quelle arance

Possessive adjectives

When followed by a plural noun, the possessive adjective also has a plural form.

i miei modelli   my models (*masc*)
le mie gonne   my skirts (*fem*)

Here is the complete list:

singular		*plural*		
masc	*fem*	*masc*	*fem*	
mio	mia	miei	mie	*my*
tuo	tua	tuoi	tue	*your (fam.)*
suo	sue	suoi	sue	*his/her/its/your*
nostro	nostra	nostri	nostre	*our*
vostro	vostra	vostri	vostre	*your*
loro	loro	loro	loro	*their*

things to do

2.4 **Vorrei una borsa bianca.** Can you tell the salesperson the color you want?

2.5 **Mi piace quest'orologio. Quanto costa?** (I like this watch. How much is it?) You are buying presents and have seen certain things you like. But you need to know how much they all cost . . .

    1 un'anello
    2 una bottiglia di profumo
    3 delle cinture
    4 una macchina fotografica
    5 delle cassette

2.6 You are in a store trying on a pair of sandals. Can you complete your part of the conversation using the words and expressions below:

non mi piace il colore/Sono troppo stretti/Sì, grazie/un paio di/ buongiorno/Posso provarli?/Numero trentanove/Questi

Commessa: Buongiorno. Cosa desidera?
You: Buongiorno. Vorrei................sandali.
Commessa: Che numero?
You: ....
Commessa: (She shows you some blue ones) Le piacciono questi?
You: Mi piace il modello ma................
Commessa: Vediamo allora. Abbiamo questi sandali anche in nero.
You: ....
Commessa: Certo. (you try them on) Le piacciono?
You: Non vanno bene. ....
Commessa: Li abbiamo nel quarantuno. Vuole provarli?
You: ....
Commessa: Come vanno?
You: ....sono un po'grandi!
Commessa: Mi dispiace (*I'm sorry*) ma non li abbiamo nel quaranta.
You: Grazie, ...

la mattina

SHOPPING – POSTCARDS AND STAMPS

Il **tabaccaio** (tobacconist) sells postage stamps **(francobolli)** as well as tobacco products (**sigarette** cigarettes), the sale of both items being state monopolies in Italy. Look for a large T-sign outside. Inside you will find that you can buy postcards **(cartoline)** and the necessary stamps to go with them, and perhaps have a drink as well, because the **tabaccheria** is often also a bar. A mailbox **(buca delle lettere)** may be red or yellow and is marked with the word **poste.**

dal tabaccaio/at the tobacco shop

Paul's in the mood for writing postcards and goes into a **tabaccheria** with Raffaella. They look at the postcards together.

Paul: **Cos'è questo?**
Raffaella: Questo è il Campanile.
Paul: È molto bello. **Prendo questa**, e questa del Duomo . . . Vorrei anche una cartolina del Ponte Vecchio. Ah! Eccola. **Quanto costano le cartoline?**
Tabaccaio: Centocinquanta l'una.

Paul: **Prendo** queste tre cartoline. **Vorrei anche tre francobolli** per la Gran Bretagna. **Quanto costa un francobollo** per una cartolina?

Tabaccaio: Quattrocentocinquanta (450) lire, signore.

Paul: Allora, tre francobolli da quattrocentocinquanta. **Quant'è in tutto?**

Tabaccaio: Sono quattrocentocinquanta (450) lire le cartoline e milletrecentocinquanta (1.350) lire i francobolli Milleottocento (1.800) lire in tutto.

Paul: (gives him a 2,000 lira note) Ecco duemila lire.

Tabaccaio: Grazie. Duecento di resto a lei.

Talking shop

Cos'è questo?	What's this?
Questo è . . .	It is/this is . . .
Prendo questa.	I'll take this one.
Vorrei anche una cartolina.	I'd also like a postcard.
un francobollo per la Gran Bretagna	a stamp for Great Britain
tre francobolli da quattrocentocinquanta	three stamps at 450 lire
ecco(lo), ecco(la)	here (it) is
Quanto costano . . .	How much are . . . ?
l'uno, l'una	each (one)
Quant'è (in tutto)?	How much is it (altogether)?
di resto a lei	change for you

SHOPPING – FOOD

Food stores are generally open from about 8:30 a.m. until 7 p.m. (or 8 p.m. in the summer). However, they close for lunch between about 1 p.m. and 3 p.m. (or 4 p.m. in the summer). You will find some open on Sundays and most shut for half a day some time during the week.

vorrei un chilo di mele/I'd like a kilo of apples

Anna and Enrico have gone shopping to buy food for the family. First they go to the fruit store (**il fruttivendolo**).

Negoziante: Buongiorno, signora, desidera?

Anna: **Vorrei un chilo di mele** rosse e **mezzo chilo di pere. Ha dell'uva bianca?** Ne vorrei un chilo e mezzo e due chili di pomodori maturi.

Negoziante: Vuole altro? Basta così? Allora—mele, pere, uva, pomodori —quattromilacinquecento lire (L4.500) in tutto.

Anna: Ecco a lei cinquemila lire (L5.000).

Negoziante: Cinquecento (L500) di resto. Arrivederci e grazie.

Next they go to the butcher's (**la macelleria**).

Negoziante: Prego, signora?

Anna: Vorrei del maiale, per favore.

Negoziante: Mi dispiace, signora, ma non ne abbiamo stamattina. Abbiamo vitello, manzo, agnello . . .

Anna: Allora, **mi dà del vitello,** per favore? Lo vorrei tenero e magro.

Negoziante: Ecco, signora. Quattro etti di carne buona. Altro?

Anna: **No, basta così.** Grazie.

Lastly they go the grocery store (**alimentari**).

Negoziante: Cosa desidera, signora?

Anna: **Ha del salame nostrano? Ne vorrei tre etti,** e poi due etti e mezzo di prosciutto crudo.

Negoziante: **Va bene così?** Altro?

Anna: Mi dà un po' di formaggio—del pecorino piccante, per favore. E vorrei anche dell'olio . . . , dello zucchero . . . , un litro di latte . . . , un chilo di caffè . . . , e sei uova.

Negoziante: Ecco a lei, signora. Basta così?

Anna: Sì, grazie. Quant'è?

Negoziante: Allora sono . . . (adding up) undici e sei—undicimilaseicento lire in totale.

Anna: Mi dà un sacchetto di plastica, per favore?

Negoziante: Certo, signora.

What the store owner might say

Cosa desidera?/Desidera?/Prego?	Can I help you?/What do you want?
Vuole altro?/Altro?	Anything else?
Basta così?	Is that enough?/Is that all?
Va bene così?	Is that OK?
Nient'altro?/Dopo?	Anything else?
Mi dispiace, non ne abbiamo.	I'm sorry, we don't have any.
stamattina/per oggi	this morning/today
Abbiamo . . .	We have . . .

25

Asking for what you want (For a list of food items see p. 81)

Vorrei . . .	I'd like . . .
un chilo di mele rosse	a kilo of red apples
mezzo chilo di pere	half a kilo of pears
Ha dell'uva bianca?	Do you have any white grapes?
Ne vorrei un chilo e mezzo.	I'd like one and a half kilos (of them).
due chili di pomodori maturi	two kilos of ripe tomatoes
Vorrei del maiale.	I'd like some pork.
Abbiamo vitello, manzo, agnello.	We have veal, beef, lamb.
Mi dà del vitello.	Give me some veal.
Lo vorrei tenero e magro.	I'd like it tender and lean.
quattro etti di carne buona	400 grams of good meat
Ha del salame nostrano?	Do you have some local salami?
della mortadella?	some spiced pork sausage?
due etti di prosciutto crudo/cotto	200 grams of cured ham/cooked ham
Che formaggio ha?	What cheese do you have?
della mozzarella/della ricotta	mild cheese for pizzas/ricotta cheese
del Bel Paese/della gorgonzola	Bel Paese/Gorgonzola (blue) cheese
dell'olio/dello zucchero	some oil/some sugar
del burro/degli spaghetti	some butter/some spaghetti
un litro di latte	a liter of milk
sei uova	half a dozen eggs
il pane	bread
del pane casereccio	homemade bread
una focaccia/un panino	flat, round loaf/bread roll
Mi dà un sacchetto di plastica.	A plastic bag please.

the way it works

Some and any

Look at the following examples:

Vorrei **del** maiale	I'd like some pork
dell'olio . . . **dello** zucchero	some oil . . . some sugar
della mozzarella/**degli spaghetti**	some mozzarrella/some spaghetti

Use the word for "of" (**di**) together with "the" (**il**, **la**, etc.). Check the table on p. 16 for the combinations of **di** and definite articles.
Note that to say "I want some of it," you use **Ne vorrei**. And if the store owner doesn't have any, the answer will be **Non ne abbiamo**.

Saying how much you want

When buying food, you will need to be able to ask for specific weights and measures. One very useful weight in Italy is the **etto** (hectogram = 100 grams). Many items can be bought by the **etto** (plural **etti**):

quattro etti di carne buona	400 grams of good meat
due etti e mezzo di salame	250 grams of salami

Other ways of specifying how much you want include:

un po' di formaggio	a little cheese
una dozzina d'uova	a dozen eggs
cinque fette di prosciutto	5 slices of ham
una bottiglia di vino	a bottle of wine
una scatola di cioccolatini	a box of chocolates
un pacchetto di sigarette	a pack of cigarettes

Paying (For numbers, see p. 78)

Understanding the amount to pay is not always easy when hundreds and thousands of lire are frequently used:

quattrocentocinquanta	450 lire	quattromilacinquecento	4.500 lire
milletrecentocinquanta	1.350 lire	undicimilaseicento	11.600 lire

You will sometimes hear a shortened form: **Undicimilaseicento lire** can also be called **undici e sei**. In other words, the words **mila** (thousands) and **cento** (hundred) are taken out and the thousands, hundreds, and units are linked by **e** (and). Thus 450 lire can be called **quattro e cinquanta**.

things to do

3.1 Before going shopping, Anna is going over in her mind all the items she needs to buy. Can you complete her list for her (using **del, dell', dello, dei, delle, degli**):

. . . pane casereccio, . . . mele e pere, . . . uva bianca, . . . pomodori, . . . maiale, . . . prosciutto, . . . spaghetti, . . . formaggio, . . . olio, . . . zucchero.

3.2 It's your turn to do the shopping! Can you ask for each item on the list starting **Mi dà** or **Vorrei**:

3.3 Can you work out in Italian the prices of the following items:

Quattro cartoline? Sono . . .   Due francobolli? Sono . . .

Un giornale inglese? È . . .   Due scatole di cioccolatini? Sono . . .

EATING OUT

Closing days   Many restaurants and bars close one day a week in turn on a rotating system **(chiusura per turno)**. In addition to the normal closing day, you may find a sign in the summer (particularly during August) which indicates holiday closing **(Chiusura estiva)**, which means the establishment could well be closed for several weeks.

Restaurants   For a full meal, choose between a **ristorante** (formal restaurant, graded by stars, forks, etc.) or a **trattoria** (medium-priced meals, often very good value). For less expensive or lighter meals look for a **rosticceria** (ready-cooked food such as spit-roasted chicken), a **tavola calda** (inexpensive hot dishes, often crowded), or, of course, a **pizzeria**, where you can either eat on the premises or buy a carry-out portion **(pizza al taglio)** to eat at home. The bill **(il conto)** usually includes a cover charge **(pane e coperto)** and service **(il servizio)**, but many people give an extra tip for really good food and service. The restaurant must give you a receipt **(una ricevuta fiscale)**, which may be checked by tax officials.

Menus   You will usually find, in addition to the à la carte dishes, a **menù a prezzo fisso** (set menu) or a **menù turistico** (tourist menu). There may be a **piatto del giorno** (special of the day) and the chef will often recommend a personal speciality—**la specialità della casa**.

cosa prendono?/what'll you have?

Raffaella is joined by her student sister, Giulia, and together with Paul they go to have lunch at a restaurant—the Olivi in Via delle Terme.

Cameriere: Buongiorno, signori, quanti sono?
Raffaella: **Siamo** tre.

Cameriere:	C'è un tavolo vicino alla finestra. (They sit down) Va bene?
Raffaella:	Sì, grazie. **Potremmo avere il menù**, per favore?
Cameriere:	Subito, signori.
	(A little later) Cosa prendono, signori?
Raffaella:	Allora, io vorrei **per primo** una minestra di funghi, e **di secondo** fegato alla veneziana.
Cameriere:	Va bene. E di contorno?
Raffaella:	**Mi porti** dei fagiolini, per favore. E per te, Giulia?
Giulia:	**A me porti** dei tortellini e una cotoletta alla milanese. **Per contorno** prendo un po'di spinaci.
Paul:	**Per me** delle fettuccine alle vongole e di secondo una bistecca alla fiorentina, per favore. E come contorno, vorrei degli zucchini e delle patate fritte.
Cameriere:	E la bistecca, come la vuole—al sangue, ben cotta?
Paul:	Al sangue.
Cameriere:	Benissimo, signore. E da bere?
Raffaella:	(to Paul) **Prendiamo** del vino bianco e anche del rosso, vero?
Paul:	Sì, va bene.
Raffaella:	**Una bottiglia** di Frascati, per favore, e anche mezzo litro di Orvieto. Oh . . . e **ci può portare anche** una bottiglia di acqua minerale?

Meals and mealtimes   Traditionally lunch **(il pranzo)** is the main meal of the day and is eaten between noon and 3 p.m. In the cities, however, many people take a shorter time for lunch and have a lighter meal. The evening meal **(la cena)** is served from about 7 or 8 p.m.

Desiderano altro? (Anything else?)

Raffaella, Giulia, and Paul have reached the dessert stage.

Cameriere:	È andato tutto bene?
Paul:	**Molto bene, grazie**.
Cameriere:	Desiderano altro? Abbiamo torta della casa, zabaglione . . .
Rafaella:	Niente dolce per me. Un caffè ristretto, per favore.
Cameriere:	E per la signorina?
Giulia:	**Avete gelati?**
Cameriere:	Sì, abbiamo cassata el gelati assortiti.
Giulia:	Una cassata **va bene per me**.
Paul:	Io vorrei del formaggio e un caffè lungo. E **posso avere il conto?**
Cameriere:	Sì, signore, lo porto subito.

Vorrei riservare un tavolo per sei.	I'd like to reserve a table for six.
Avete un tavolo per quattro?	Do you have a table for four?
un'altra sedia?	another chair?
Quanti sono?	How many are you?
un tavolo vicino alla finestra	a table near the window
. . . sulla terrazza/all'angolo	. . . on the terrace/in the corner

Ordering a meal

Potremmo avere il menù?	Can we have the menu?
Cosa consiglia?	What do you recommend?
antipasti	hors d'oeuvres
primi piatti/secondi piatti	first courses/second courses
per primo/come secondo	as a first course/for second course
Vorrei una frittata	I'd like an omelette
. . . di spinaci/di formaggio	. . . spinach/cheese
contorni/desserts	vegetables/desserts
verdure di stagione/contorno a scelta	vegetables in season/choice of vegetables
per contorno/come dessert	as a vegetable/for dessert
È possibile avere . . . ?	Is it possible to have . . . ?
Anche per te?	For you too?
La prendo anch'io.	I'll have it too.
Come sono gli spaghetti?	How is the spaghetti prepared?
La bistecca, come la vuole?	How do you like your steak?
al sangue/ben cotta	rare/well done
Da bere?	What would you like to drink?
una bottiglia di/mezzo litro di	a bottle of/a half liter of
Ci può portare . . . ?	Could you bring us . . . ?
acqua minerale	mineral water
Niente dolce per me.	Nothing sweet for me.
Avete gelati?	Do you have ice cream?
Abbiamo cassata.	We have cassata. (ice cream with candied fruit)
gelati assortiti	various flavors of ice cream
alla fragola/al limone/alla vaniglia	strawberry/lemon/vanilla flavor
Vorrei del formaggio.	I'd like some cheese.
torta di cioccolata	chocolate cake
Prendo un caffè ristretto	I'll have a strong black coffee
un caffè lungo	large weaker black coffee
Posso avere il conto?	Please could I have the bill?
Dove sono i gabinetti?	Where are the toilets?

Posso avere un coltello? (May I have a knife?)

the way it works

Ways of asking for something to be brought

Note the following:

Per me . . .	For me . . .
Mi porti . . .	Bring me . . .

Also:

Posso avere . . . ?	Could I have . . . ?
Ci può portare . . . ?	Could you bring us . . . ?
Potremmo avere . . . ?	Could we have . . . ?

Direct object pronouns (1)

La bistecca? Come **la** vuole?	The steak? How do you want it (done)?
Il conto? **Lo** porto subito.	The bill? I'll bring it at once.

The word for "it" is **lo** for a masculine noun and **la** for a feminine noun. In the plural use **li** and **le** for "them." Note also that **lo, la, li, le** can refer to people as well as objects.

Object pronouns usually come *before* the verb:

Il cameriere? **Lo** vedo.	The waiter? I see him.

The full list of unstressed direct object pronouns is as follows:

singular		*plural*	
mi	me	ci	us
ti	you (familiar)	vi	you
la	you (formal)	le	you (formal)
lo	him/it	li	them (masc.)
la	her/it	le	them (fem.)

Direct object pronouns (2)

This group of pronouns is used only after a word such as **a** or **per**.

Per **me** va bene.	That's fine for me.
Anche per **te?**	And for you, too?

singular		*plural*	
me	me	noi	us
te	you (familiar)	voi	you (familiar)
lei	you (formal)/her	loro	you (formal)/them
lui	him		

Note that with the exception of **me** and **te**, they are identical to the subject pronouns.

Regular verbs: group 2 (prendere)

The verb **prendere** (to have or take) is an example of the second group of regular Italian verbs (infinite **-ere**). Here is its full pattern in the present tense:

singular		*plural*	
prend**o**	I take	prend**iamo**	we take
prend**i**	you take (familiar)	prend**ete**	you take
prend**e**	he/she/it takes, you take (formal)	prend**ono**	he/she/it takes, you take (formal)

"You" in the plural

In the singular there is a clear distinction between the use of the **tu** and **lei** forms. In contrast, in the plural the difference in usage is not so great. The second person (**voi**) form is more frequently used than the third, even if you are using the **lei** form in the singular. The third person plural (**loro**) is formal, but is often used by waiters, etc.

things to do

3.4 Sitting at your restaurant table, you find you need to ask for quite a few things. Use **Avete . . . ?** or **Mi porti . . .**

1 Could you please have another chair.
2 You'd like the salt and pepper.
3 You want to know if they have roast chicken on the menu.
4 You want to know if they have french fries.

3.5 You arrive at a restaurant with two friends.

Waiter:	Buona sera, quanti sono?
You:	[Say you are three. Ask if he has a table on the terrace]
Waiter:	Sì. Questo tavolo va bene?
You:	[Yes, that's fine.]
Waiter:	Cosa prendono, signori?
You:	[For the lady: fish soup and a veal cutlet in marsala sauce] [For the gentleman: tagliatelle with clams and a grilled steak] [For yourself: baked cannelloni and chicken breasts]
Waiter:	Va bene, e per contorni?
You:	[Ask him to bring some courgettes (zucchini), some mushrooms, and some beans]
Waiter:	E da bere?
You:	[Say you'd like a bottle of Orvieto and a half liter of mineral water]
Waiter:	Subito, signori.

MENÙ

Antipasti:

Insalata di frutti di mare	Seafood salad
Prosciutto con melone	Cured ham and melon

Primi piatti:

Minestra di funghi	Mushroom soup
Spaghetti alla carbonara	Spaghetti with egg & bacon
Tortellini al pomodoro	Small, stuffed pasta with tomato sauce
Tagliatelle alla vongole	Tagliatelle with clams
Cannelloni al forno	Baked cannelloni

Second piatti:

Cotolette alla romana	Veal cutlet in marsala sauce
Pollo alla caccaitora	Chicken in wine sauce with onions, tomatoes, peppers, etc
Bistecca alla fiorentina	Grilled steak with pepper
Fegato alla veneziana	Calves liver fried with onions

Contorni:

Zucchini/Fagiolini/Spinaci	Zucchini/string beans/ Spinach
Insalata mista/verde	Mixed green salad

BANKS AND CURRENCY EXCHANGE

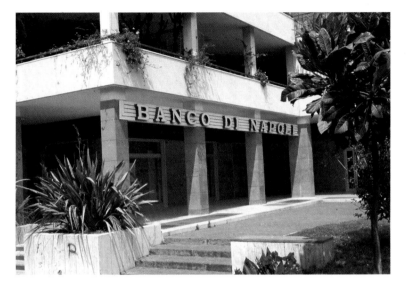

Banks are open Monday through Friday except on public holidays. The hours are from about 8:30 or 9 a.m. till about 12:30 or 1 p.m. They are sometimes open for an hour in the afternoon between about 3 and 4 p.m. Traveler's checks are accepted by some hotels and many shops, but you will get a better rate of exchange at a bank.

Money   Paper currency **(i bigletti)** comes in denominations of 500, 1,000, 2,000, 5,000, 10,000, 50,000, and 100,000 lire. There are coins of 10, 20, 50, 100, 200, and 500 lire. Credit cards are widely accepted as a method of paying in hotels, restaurants, and stores, but not in gas stations.

vado in banca/I'm going to the bank

Paul wants to go to Venice the next day for a music festival, and Giulia is going with him. She has come to see Paul, who has plans for the morning.

Giulia:	Ciao, Paul. **Cosa fai** stamattina?
Paul:	Prima **vado in banca** e poi alla Stazione Centrale. **Vado a fare il bigletto** per Venezia per domani mattina.
Giulia:	Posso accompagnarti?
Paul:	Certo!
(They arrive at the bank)	
Impiegato:	Desidera, signore?

Paul: Buongiorno. **Vorrei incassare questi tre traveler's checks. Quant'è il cambio della sterlina?**

Impiegato: La sterlina è a duemila lire. Mi dà il suo passaporto, per favore. (Paul hands it over) . . . E firmi qui . . . Grazie. Come vuole i soldi?

Paul: Vorrei **un biglietto da ventimila** e due da cinquemila. (Clerk gives him the money) Grazie.

Impiegato: Prego.

USEFUL WORDS AND PHRASES

Cosa fai stamattina?	What are you doing this morning?
primo . . . poi	first . . . then
Vado in banca/alla stazione.	I'm going to the bank/to the station.
Vado a fare il biglietto.	I'm going to buy a ticket.
domani mattina	tomorrow morning
Posso accompagnarti?	Can I come with you?
Certo!	Certainly, with pleasure!

At the bank

Vorrei incassare . . .	I'd like to cash . . .
. . . questo traveler's check	. . . this traveler's check
Mi può cambiare . . . ?	Can you change . . . ?
. . . cento dollari	. . . $100
. . . un assegno (di conto corrente)	. . . a personal check
Ho una carta di credito.	I have a credit card.
Quant'è il cambio della sterlina?	What is the exchange rate of the pound?
Il dollaro è a . . .	The dollar is at . . .
Firmi qui.	Sign here.
Come vuole i soldi?	How do you want your money?
un biglietto da ventimila	one 20,000 lire note
Vorrei aprire un conto	I want to open an account
versare questo	deposit this
prelevare . . . lire	withdraw . . . lire
Ha degli spiccioli?	Do you have any small change?

PUBLIC TRANSPORTATION: TRAINS

Trains   Train travel is generally cheap and comfortable in Italy. There are many different types of train and variations in fares, so it is worth being specific when asking for information. The main types are as follows:

Super-rapido or TEE: Luxury first-class-only trains running between main Italian cities. You pay a supplement and you must reserve a seat.
Rapido: Fast intercity trains, some of which are first-class only. You pay a supplement and for some trains it is obligatory to reserve a seat.
Expresso: Long-distance trains stopping at main stations. Both classes.
Diretto: Trains stopping at most stations.
Locale: Trains stopping at all stations.

Children under four travel free and from four to twelve pay half fare. There are several forms of reduced fare available to tourists, both individually and in groups.

Metro   There are underground networks **(la metropolitana)** in Rome and Milan. Fares are based on a flat rate, no matter what the distance traveled.

a che ora parte?/what time does it leave?

Next, Paul and Giulia go to the station. Paul asks a passerby how to get there.

Paul:	Scusi, **come si fa per andare alla stazione** centrale?
Passante:	Va a piedi, vero? Così fa più presto. Allora, prenda la Via dei Serragli, passi per la Piazza Goldoni e vada sempre diritto.
Paul:	Grazie.

Arriving at the station, Paul and Giulia go to the information office
(**l'ufficio informazioni**) to find out the times of the trains to Venice.

Paul: Buongiorno. **Vorrei sapere l'orario dei treni** per Venezia. **C'è un treno diretto**, o devo cambiare?

Impiegata: È diretto. Quando vuole partire?

Paul: **Domani mattina.**

Impiegata: Domani mattina? C'è un rapido che parte alle dieci e venticinque. Arriva a Venezia alle tredici e trentasette.

Paul: **Quanto costa il biglietto?**

Impiegata: Andata o andata e ritorno?

Paul: Solo **andata, seconda classe.**

Impiegata: Allora sono dodicimilaseicento lire.

Paul: **C'è vettura ristorante?**

Impiegata: Sì, signore.

How does one get there?

Come si fa per andare a . . . ?	How does one get to . . . ?
va a piedi	you are walking
Così (lei) fa più presto.	You'll get there more quickly.

Next they go to the ticket office.

Paul: **Mi dà due biglietti di andata sul rapido** di domani mattina per Venezia, per favore?

Impiegato: In prima o seconda classe?

Paul: Seconda.

Impiegato: Va bene. (He gives Paul the ticket) Dodicimilaseicento lire.

Paul: (He pays) Il **treno parte alle dieci** e venticinque, vero?

Impiegato: Esatto.

Paul: **Su che binario arriva?**

Impiegato: Sul primo binario.

Train inquiries

Vorrei sapere l'orario . . .	I'd like to find out the schedule . . .
. . . dei treni per Venezia	. . . of trains to Venice
C'è un treno diretto?	Is there a direct train?
Devo cambiare?	Do I have to change?
C'è una coincidenza per . . . ?	Is there a connection to . . . ?
Si ferma a Palermo.	It stops at Palermo.
Quando vuole viaggiare?	When do you want to travel?
domani mattina	tomorrow morning
Quando parte il prossimo treno per . . . ?	When is the next train to . . . ?
C'è un rapido.	There's a *rapido*.
Il treno parte a . . .	The train leaves at . . .
A che ora arriva a Venezia?	What time does it arrive in Venice?

Torno in giornata
   dopodomani
	I'm coming back the same day
	   the day after tomorrow

C'è vettura ristorante?	Is there a dining car?
Su che binario arriva?	What track does it come in on?

Buying a train ticket

Mi dà due biglietti per . . .	I'd like two tickets to . . .
un biglietto chilometrico	reduced ticket valid for 3,000 km
metà tariffa	half fare
andata/andata e ritorno	one-way/round-trip ticket
prima classe/seconda classe	first/second class
Vorrei prenotare un posto.	I'd like to reserve a seat.

Attenzione! Attenzione! (Listen for the following phrases)

È in arrivo sul binario quattro . . .	Arriving on track 4 . . .
il treno da . . .	the train from . . .
il treno per . . .	the train for . . .
Ha circa cinque minuti di ritardo.	It's about 5 minutes late.
L'arrivo è previsto alle . . .	It's expected to arrive at . . .

the way it works

Cosa fai? (What are you doing?)

Fare (to do, make) is also used in many colloquial phrases:

Vado a **fare** il biglietto.	I'm going to buy a ticket.
Come **si fa** per . . . ?	How does one get to . . .? (lit. one do?)

The present tense of this verb is irregular:

faccio	I do, make	**facciamo**	we do, make
fai	you do (familiar)	**fate**	you do
fa	he/she does, you do (formal)	**fanno**	they do, you do (formal)

Vado . . .

We have already met several phrases which use parts of the verb **andare** (to go).

Vado in banca.	I'm going to the bank.
Va bene.	OK. (lit. it goes well)
Andiamo a casa.	We are going home.

Like **fare**, the present tense of this verb is irregular:

vado	I go	**andiamo**	we go
vai	you go (familiar)	**andate**	you go
va	he/she goes, you go (formal)	**vanno**	they go, you go (formal)

Impersonal si

To say "How does one . . . ?" you use **Come si . . . ? Si** is used frequently in Italian to mean "one" or "you" or "people" in general.

Come **si** dice questo in italiano?	How does one say this in Italian?
Si può parcheggiare qui?	Can one park here?

Regular verbs: group 3 (partire)

You will need the verb **partire** (to leave) when talking about traveling:
A che ora **parte** il prossimo treno?   What time does the next train leave?
It is an example of the third category (infinitive **-ire**) of Italian verbs:

part**o**	I leave	part**iamo**	we leave
part**i**	you leave (familiar)	part**ite**	you leave
part**e**	he/she/it leaves, you leave (formal)	part**ono**	they leave, you leave (formal)

things to do

4.1 You are in a bank and you want to change some money.

You: [Say good morning. You'd like to change £50 pounds]
Clerk: Ha il passaporto, per favore?
You: [Yes, here it is. Ask what the exchange rate is]
Clerk: È a duemilatrecento lire. Firmi qui, per favore e passi alla cassa. Vuole un biglietto da centomila?
You: [No. Ask to be given two L50,000 bills]
Clerk: Ecco a lei. Grazie e buongiorno.

4.2 You overhear a railroad employee advising a passenger about trains. Can you guess what the passenger is saying?

Passenger: . . . . ?
Clerk: Il prossimo treno per Siena parte alle quattordici e dieci.
Passenger: . . . . ?
Clerk: Deve cambiare a Chiusi.
Passenger: . . . . ?
Clerk: Arriva a Siena alle diciannove e trenta.
Passenger: . . . . ?
Clerk: Andata o andata e ritorno?
Passenger: . . . .

4.3 A che ora parte il treno per . . . ? You are at the train station in Milan with a group of tourists, each of whom wants to go to a different Italian city. Can you say when each train leaves and when it arrives?

	PARTENZE	ARRIVI
Bologna	9:15	11:45
Torino	10:20	12:50
Firenze	11:30	15:30
Ancona	12:02	18:00
Roma	13:40	21:30

PUBLIC TRANSPORTATION: BUSES

L'autobus   Buses are the only form of public transportation in most Italian cities. Fares are normally charged on a flat-rate basis. The method of buying tickets varies. For example, in some places, you pay on the bus, but in Milan and Rome, you have to buy tickets in advance at a newsstand. Sometimes you pay at the bus stop either by putting the exact change into a ticket dispenser or by putting a special ticket **(una tesserina)**, bought at a newsstand, into a hole-punching machine.

Il pullman (coach), **la corriera** (country bus): There is an extensive coach and bus network covering every part of Italy.

per andare a . . .?/how do I get to . . .?

Marisa decides to visit a famous church on a hill outside Florence. She asks a passerby for advice:

Marisa:	Per piacere, **per andare** a San Miniato al Monte, **devo prendere l'autobus?**
Passante:	Sì, signorina. Deve prendere il 13 e scendere al Piazzale Michelangelo.
Marisa:	**Mi può dire dov'è la fermata** del 13, per favore?
Passante:	Allora . . . Vada fino al semaforo. Attraversi la strada e giri a destra. La fermata è lì sulla destra.
Marisa:	Ho capito. **Ogni quanto passano gli autobus?**

Passante:	Ogni dieci minuti, credo.
Marisa:	E mi può dire **quanto tempo ci mette?**
Passante:	Circa quindici minuti . . . Non lo so esattamente.
Marisa:	Grazie mille.
Passante:	Prego.

Going by bus

Dov'è la stazione degli autobus?	Where is the bus station?
Devo prendere l'autobus?	Should I take the bus?
C'è un autobus?	Is there a bus?
Che numero devo prendere?	What number should I take?
Deve prendere il 13 e scendere a . . .	You should take the 13 and get off at . . .
Dov'è la fermata del 13?	Where is the No. 13 bus stop?
Vada fino al semaforo.	Go to the traffic lights.
Attraversi la strada.	Cross the street.
Giri a destra.	Turn right.
La fermata si trova sulla destra.	The stop is on the right.
Sa ogni quanto passano?	Do you know how often they run?
Ogni venti minuti, credo.	Every 20 minutes, I think.
Mi può dire . . . ?	Can you tell me?
. . . quanto tempo ci mette?	. . . how long it (the trip) takes?
circa quindici minuti	about 15 minutes
Non lo so esattamente.	I don't know exactly.
Mi può dire quando devo scendere?	Can you tell me when to get off?
Questa è la fermata per . . . ?	Is this the stop for . . . ?
Questo pullman si ferma a . . . ?	Does this coach stop at . . . ?
Quest'autobus va a . . . ?	Does this bus go to . . . ?

(For departure times, etc., see section on Train Inquiries, p. 36)

TELEPHONE

Telephones Telephone calls can be made from hotels and from public phones, including phone booths **(la cabina telefonica)**. You can also make local calls from a café, where you sometimes need a token **(un gettone)**. You will also find a large number of public phones that accept magnetic telephone cards **(la scheda magnetica/carta telefonica)**. These cards are available at offices of the SIP (the name of the Italian telephone system).

che ne pensi?/what do you think?

Back in the Lazzarinis' flat that evening, Giancarlo telephones a friend on the island of Elba to ask if he and Marisa can go and visit him this weekend.

Marco:	**Pronto?**
Giancarlo:	**Qui parla** Giancarlo. Come stai, Marco?
Marco:	Bene, grazie, e tu?
Giancarlo:	**Benissimo**. Senti, Marco, Marisa e io pensiamo di visitarvi questo finesettimana. **Che ne pensi?**
Marco:	**Ottima idea!** Quando venite?
Giancarlo:	Domani sera—non so esattamente quando. Di passaggio vogliamo fermarci a Siena per pranzare e vedere le cose più interessanti. Prendiamo il traghetto alle cinque circa. Non mi ricordo quanto tempo ci mette . . .
Marco:	Circa un'ora. Va bene. **Allora a domani.**
Giancarlo:	Arriverderci.

Making plans

pensiamo di . . .	we are thinking of . . .
visitarvi	visiting you
questo finesettimana	this weekend
Ottima idea!	Brilliant idea!
Quando venite?	When are you coming?
domani sera	tomorrow evening
di passaggio	en route
Vogliamo fermarci per pranzare.	We want to stop for lunch.
Prendiamo il traghetto.	We'll take the ferry.
Non mi ricordo . . .	I don't remember . . .
. . . quanto tempo ci mette	. . . how long it takes

Telephone talk

Dov'è la cabina telefonica più vicina?	Where's the nearest phone booth?
Vorrei un gettone.	I want a token.
Qual'è il prefisso per . . . ?	What's the area code for . . . ?
Mi può dare il numero di . . . ?	Can you tell me the number for . . . ?
Desidero il 40 25 58 di Roma.	I want Rome 40 25 58.
un elenco telefonico	a telephone directory
Pronto. Sono . . .	Hello (*answering*) I am . . .
Qui parla . . .	This is . . . speaking.
Chi parla?	Who's speaking?
Vorrei parlare a . . .	I want to speak to . . .
Un momento. Resti in linea.	One moment. Hold on.
Può passare un messaggio?	Can you pass on a message?
Ha chiamato il numero sbagliato.	You've got the wrong number.
Il telefono non funziona.	The phone isn't working.

the way it works

Means of transportation

Note that in Italian you say **a piedi** (on foot). However, most forms of transportation are preceded by **in**:

Vado **in** autobus	I'm going by bus	Vado **in** macchina	I'm going by car
in aereo	by plane	**in** taxi	by taxi
in bicicletta	by bicycle	**in** treno	by train
in corriera	by bus, coach	**in** traghetto	by ferry

Where are you going?

Dove va per le vacanze? Vado **in** Italia. (with names of countries)
Vado **a** Firenze. (with names of towns, etc.)

Asking someone to do something for you

Note the expression **Mi può dire . . . ?** (Can you tell me . . . ?) **Mi può** can be used with a variety of expressions:
Mi può cambiare questo traveler's check?
Mi può dare un biglietto?
Può is part of the verb **potere** (to be able), whose present tense is as follows:

posso	I can	**possiamo**	we can
puoi	you can (familiar)	**potete**	you can
può	he/she/it can, you can (formal)	**possono**	they can, you can (formal)

Giving instructions

Not only will you want to be able to ask the way and understand directions, but you might also need to be able to give simple instructions yourself.

We have already met (Martedì mattina) words like **prenda** (take), **vada** (go), **giri** (turn), **passi per** (go along), which are forms of the verb known as the imperative (or command) form. Here we meet one more: **attraversi** (cross). The imperative is formed with the stem of the first person "I" form and the following endings:
Regular **-are** verbs: **-i**
Regular **-ere** and **-ire** verbs: **-a**
Note one other way in which you may be told politely what to do.
Deve prendere il autobus.   You must take the bus.
Deve is part of the verb **dovere** (to have to, must):

devo	I must	**dobbiamo**	we must
devi	you must (familiar)	**dovete**	you must
deve	he/she must, you must (formal)	**devono**	they must, you must (formal)

Reflexive verbs

Non mi ricordo (I don't remember) is an example of a verb which is being used reflexively, i.e., the subject acts upon, or does something to, himself or herself.

Ricordare means "to remind" and thus the reflexive form **ricordarsi** means "to remind oneself" or "to remember." The reflexive is formed by the addition of a special set of reflexive pronouns which, except in the infinitive, come before the verb, as follows:

mi ricordo	I remember	**ci** ricordiamo	we remember
ti ricordi	you remember (fam)	**vi** ricordate	you remember
si ricorda	he/she remembers, you remember (formal)	**si** ricordano	they remember, you remember (formal)

Reflexive pronouns in some cases may be translated into English as "oneself," etc.:
lavarsi = to wash (oneself); **mi lavo** = I wash (myself).
sposari = to marry (someone); **incontrarsi** = to meet (one another)

things to do

4.4 Dove va in vacanza? Where are you going for your holiday this year? Everyone is going somewhere different, and by a different means:

Carla: Inghilterra   Antonio: Napoli

Leo: Francia   Giulia: Orvieto

4.5 At the bus station, you inquire about coaches to Milan.

Bigliettaio:	Buongiorno. Desidera?
You:	[Ask if there is a coach to Milan]
Bigliettaio:	Sì, ogni trenta minuti.
You:	[Ask when the next coach to Milan leaves]
Bigliettaio:	Parte alle undici en trenta.
You:	[Ask how long it takes]
Bigliettaio:	Circa quattro ore.
You:	[Ask how much the ticket costs]
Bigliettaio:	Andata o andata e ritorno?
You:	[Single (one-way)]
Bigliettaio:	Sono duemilaquattrocento.
You:	[OK. Say you want a single (one-way) ticket]

4.6 Come si fa per andare alla posta? Can you tell people how to get to various places?

1 La posta?	[Take the first street on the right and it's on the left.]
2 La Banca Commerciale?	[Go to the traffic lights and cross the road. It's just there, on the right.]
3 Fiesole	[You must take the bus. It takes about one hour. The stop is in the Piazza della Repubblica.]

43

DRIVING THE CAR

Documents   To drive in Italy, you need either an international driver's license or a translation of your U.S. driver's license. To rent a car in Italy, you typically need to show only your U.S. driver's license and your passport. The Automobile Club of Italy (ACI) offers services similar to those of American automobile clubs. It has offices in most Italian towns.

Gasoline   Gasoline is expensive in Italy, as in many other European counties. Discount coupons are available to foreign drivers. These can be obtained at offices of the ACI at major airports, such as the ones in Rome and in Milan. To obtain blocks of these gasoline coupons, you have to pay in Italian currency.

Breakdowns   If you do break down, dial 116 at the nearest telephone, tell the operator your whereabouts and the registration number and make of your car, and the ACI will come to your assistance. All vehicles must carry a yellow warning triangle which should be placed at least 50 meters behind the car.

Highway code   Italy adheres to the International Highway Code. It is compulsory to have a side mirror fitted on the left-hand side of the car. The wearing of seat belts is strongly recommended. Note the following speed limits (for cars):

	to 600cc	to 900cc	to 1300cc	over 1300cc
Towns and villages:	50 km/h	50 km/h	50 km/h	50 km/h
Country roads:	80	90	100	110
Highways:	90	110	130	140

Some Italian road signs

Senso Vietato } Vietato l'Acceso }	No entry
Sosta Vietata } Divieto di Sosta }	No parking
Rallentare	Slow down
Svolta	Bend
Lavori Stradale	Road repairs
Senso Unico	One-way street
Zona di Silenzio	No honking
Precedenza a destra	Priority to vehicles coming from the right
Passaggio a Livello	Level crossing
Divieto di Sorpasso	No passing
Sosta Autorizzata	Parking permitted (within certain times)
Deviazione	Detour
Incrocio	Crossroads
Uscita/Entrata	Exit/Entrance
Soccorso ACI	ACI emergency service
Parcheggio limitato	Limited parking

Highways   Italian highways (**autostrade**) are well engineered and cover most of the country, often running through spectacular scenery. The **Autostrada del Sole** (A1), which runs from Milan to Reggio di Calabria, is nearly 900 miles long. You collect a ticket at the entrance to the highway and at your exit you pay a toll (**pedaggio**) which is based on the engine size of your car and the distance covered.

Parking   In the center of towns, parking is limited, and you will find that in blue zones you have to display a parking disk (**disco di sosta**) which you set to show the time you arrived. These are available from gas stations.

Breakdowns and repairs (For a list of parts of the car, see p. 82)

Ho un guasto alla macchina.	My car has broken down.
La mia macchina non parte	My car won't start
. . . non funziona molto bene	. . . isn't working
Il motore surriscalda.	The engine is overheating.
Dov'è il garage più vicino?	Where's the nearest garage?
Può mandare un meccanico?	Can you send a mechanic?
Sono rimasto senza benzina.	I've run out of gas.
Può riparare questa gomma?	Can you repair this tire?
RIPARAZIONE GOMME	TIRE REPAIRS
Potrebbe cambiare le candele?	Could you change the plugs?
Il mio numero di immatricolazione è . . .	My registration number is . . .

45

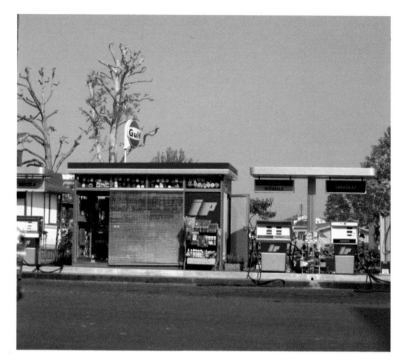

il pieno, per favore/fill it up, please

On the way to Siena, Giancarlo and Marisa stop for gas.

Marisa: Che caldo! Che ne dici di fermarci a bere qualcosa?

Giancarlo: Bè . . . Abbiamo bisogno di benzina. Cerco una stazione di servizio. (Suddenly he sees one) Ah! ce n'è una, là sulla destra.

(He drives in and stops)

Benzinaio: Quanti litri, signore?

Giancarlo: **Mi faccia il pieno**, per favore.

Benzinaio: Normale o super?

Giancarlo: **Super.** (The tank is filled) E **mi può controllare l'olio**, per piacere?

Benzinaio: Senz'altro. (He checks the oil) È un po'basso. Ne aggiungo un litro.

Giancarlo: Grazie. Mi può guardare anche l'acqua?

Benzinaio: L'acqua è a posto.

Giancarlo: Va bene. Allora quant'è?

Benzinaio: Quarantamilanovecento.

Giancarlo: Ecco a lei cinquantamila.

Benzinaio: Benissimo. Grazie e arrivederci.

Abbiamo bisogno di benzina.	We need gas.
una stazione di servizio	a service station
Quanti litri?	How many liters?
quaranta litri	40 liters
(Mi faccia) il pieno.	Fill it up.
normale o super	regular or premium
la benzina senza piombo	lead-free gas
il gasolio	diesel
Mi può controllare l'olio?	Could you check the oil for me?
. . . la pressione delle gomme	. . . the tire pressure
senz'altro	of course
È un po'basso.	It's a bit low.
Ne aggiungo un litro.	I'll put in a liter.
(Tutto) a posto.	(All) in order, OK.

USEFUL WORDS AND PHRASES

Che caldo!	How hot it is!
Che ne dici di . . . ?	How about . . . ?
bere qualcosa	to have something to drink
Cerco . . .	I'm looking for . . .
Ce n'è una.	Here's one.

LOSS AND THEFT

ho perso il portafoglio/I have lost my wallet

They set off again and haven't gone far before Marisa makes an unwelcome discovery . . .

Marisa: Oh, no! Mi dispiace, Giancarlo, **ho perso il portafoglio**. Credo di averlo lasciato nella stazione di servizio.

(Giancarlo stops the car)

Giancarlo: Ma come hai fatto a perderlo?

Marisa: Non sono sicura . . . Non mi ricordo.

Giancarlo: **Hai comprato una bibita?**

Marisa: Ah! Sì. Adesso mi ricordo. Ho comprato una bibita, e **ho messo** il portafoglio sulla cassa. Poi ho dimenticato di rimetterlo nella borsa.

Giancarlo: Non preoccuparti, non importa, ci torniamo subito. Anch'io ho fatto lo stesso **una settimana fa!** Ho perso tutte le carte di credito e non le ho più trovate.

47

I have lost . . . !

Ho perso il portafoglio.	I've lost my purse/wallet.
l'ho lasciato	I have left it
Come hai fatto a perderlo?	How did you lose it?
Non sono sicura.	I'm not sure.
Hai comprato una bibita?	Did you buy a drink?
Ho comprato . . .	I bought . . .
Ho messo il portafoglio sulla cassa.	I put the purse by the cash register.
Ho dimenticato di rimetterlo.	I forgot to put it back.
Ci torniamo subito.	We'll go back at once.
Ho fatto lo stesso.	I did the same thing.
una settimana fa	a week ago
Ho perso tutte le carte di credito.	I lost all my credit cards.
Non le ho più trovate.	I haven't found them.
Mi è stato rubato il portafoglio	My wallet has been stolen
. . . la macchina fotografica	. . . my camera
. . . i miei oggetti di valore	. . . my valuables
Ho bisogno di fare la denuncia.	I need to report to the police.
Chiami la polizia!	Call the police!

USEFUL WORDS AND PHRASES

Mi dispiace.	I'm sorry.
Non preoccuparti.	Don't worry.
Non importa.	It doesn't matter.

the way it works

Saying what you did

When talking about a past action, you use the perfect tense:
Hai comprato una bibita?   Did you buy a drink?
The perfect tense is formed by using part of the present tense of **avere** or **essere**
followed by a past participle of the verb. Some verbs are preceded by **avere** and
others by **essere**. Past participles are formed as follows:

-are verbs   drop **-are** and add **-ato**: comprare, comprato (bought)
-ire verbs   drop **-ire** and add **-ito**:   partire, partito (left)
-ere verbs have no regular pattern—learn each one separately:

bere (to drink):	bevuto	perdere (to lose):	perso
dovere (must, ought):	dovuto	prendere (to take):	preso
mettere (to put):	messo	volere (to want):	voluto

The perfect tense (using avere)

The majority of Italian verbs form their perfect tense with **avere**. Here is an example of the pattern of the perfect tense:

ho comprato	I (have) bought	abbiamo comprato	we (have) bought
hai comprato	you (have) bought (familiar)	avete comprato	you (have) bought
ha comprato	he/she (has) bought you (have) bought (formal)	hanno comprato	they (have) bought you (have) bought (formal)

The ending of the past participle of these verbs is -o and does not change except when there is a feminine or plural object pronoun before it. These are **la, l'** (before a vowel or **h**), **li, le**:
Dov'è la borsa? **L'**ho mess**a** sulla tavola. (fem. singular)*
Ho perso tutte le carte di credito e non **le** ho più trovat**e**. (fem. plural)
***L'** may be masculine or feminine, but the participle only changes its ending if the noun to which it refers is feminine.

How to say you need something

Abbiamo bisogno di benzina.   We need gas.
To express a need, use a part of the verb **avere + bisogno** (which doesn't change).
Ho bisogno di una gomma.   I need a tire.

things to do

5.1 You are at a service station. Say to the attendant in Italian:
   1 that you want unleaded petrol (gas)
   2 that you'd like 30 liters
   3 ask him to check the oil
   4 thank him and ask how much it is

5.2 You see the following three street signs. What do they mean?
   1 **Senso Vietato**
      (a) No Parking   (b) No Entry   (c) One-Way Street
   2 **Sosta Vietata**
      (a) Road Repairs   (b) No Parking   (c) Parking Permitted
   3 **Divieto di Sorpasso**
      (a) Detour   (b) No Entry   (c) No Passing

5.3 You can't find your camera and you go back to a café where you had a drink earlier.
   Direttore: Buona sera, signore. Desidera?
   You: [You are sorry, but you think you left your camera here]
   Direttore: L'ha lasciata qui? Dove l'ha messa, signore?
   You: [Say you put the camera down on the table, bought a drink, and then forgot to pick it up afterwards]
   Direttore: Un attimo . . . (he goes to look) Ce n'è una qui. È questa?
   You: [Say yes, that's yours and thank him very much]

ILLNESS AND ACCIDENT

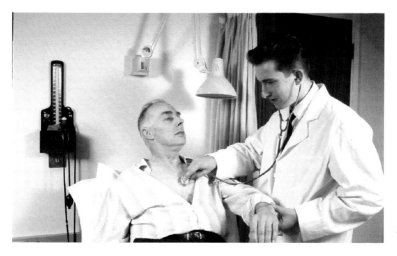

Health You might want to purchase traveler's insurance before leaving for Italy. Check with your insurance agent. In case of minor injuries or illnesses, you will usually find that the pharmacist is very helpful. Pharmacists in Italy may sell and recommend medicine that is often available in the U.S. only by prescription.

mi sento male/I feel ill

Giancarlo's father, Enrico, hasn't been feeling well and goes to the doctor.

Medico: Buongiorno, signore. Si sieda qui.
Enrico: **Non mi sento molto bene,** dottore. **Mi fa male il torace.**
Medico: Da quanto tempo le fa male?
Enrico: Non sono sicuro. **Da circa due settimane . . .**
Medico: Ha la febbre?
Enrico: No, penso di no. Ma **ho mal di gola** e ho anche la tosse.
(The doctor examines his throat and chest)
Medico: Apra la bocca . . . grazie. Adesso respiri profondamente . . . Ancora . . . Va bene. Lei ha una bronchite. Le prescrivo un antibiotico. È allergico alla penicillina?
Enrico: No.
Medico: (writes a prescription) Allora, ecco un ricetta. Prenda una compressa tre volte al giorno prima di ogni pasto.

Enrico: Grazie, dottore.

Diagnosis . . . *(For parts of the body, see p. 81–82)*

Si sieda qui.	Sit down here.
Non mi sento molto bene.	I don't feel very well.
Mi sento male.	I feel sick.
Dove fa male?	Where does it hurt?
Mi fa male il torace.	My chest is hurting.
Mi fa male il/la . . .	My . . . hurts.
Da quanto tempo le fa male il . . . ?	How long has your . . . been hurting?
Da quanto tempo si sente male?	How long have you been feeling ill?
da circa due settimane	for about two weeks
Ha la febbre?	Do you have a temperature?
Penso di no.	I don't think so.
Ho mal di gola . . . e ho la tosse.	I have a sore throat . . . and a cough.
Ho la diarrea.	I have diarrhea.
Ho vomitato.	I've been sick.
Apra la bocca.	Open your mouth.
Respiri profondamente.	Breathe deeply.
ancora	again
Lei ha una bronchite.	You have bronchitis.

. . . and prescription

Le prescrivo . . .	I'll prescribe . . .
. . . un antibiotico	. . . an antibiotic
Lei è allergico alla penicillina?	Are you allergic to penicillin?
Sono allergico agli antibiotici.	I'm allergic to antibiotics.
Che medicina prende?	What medicine are you on?
Sono incinta (di 3 mesi).	I'm (3 months) pregnant.
Prendo la pillola.	I'm on the pill.
Ho il diabete.	I have diabetes.
Deve andare all'ospedale.	You must go to the hospital.
Voglio che faccia una radiografia.	I'd like you to have an X ray.
Deve restare a letto.	You must stay in bed.
Ecco una ricetta.	Here's a prescription.
Prenda una compressa . . .	Take one pill . . .
tre volte al giorno	three times a day
prima di/dopo ogni pasto	before/after meals

Pharmacies   Pharmacies have a green or red cross outside and so are easily recognized. At every shop, there is a list of those in the vicinity which are open at night or on Sundays.

At the pharmacist's *(For pharmaceutical items, see p. 80)*

Può darmi qualcosa per . . . ?	Can you give me something for . . . ?
. . . la febbre da fieno	. . . hay fever
. . . le puncture d'insetti	. . . insect bites
Sono stato punto.	I've been stung.
Ho un taglio/una contusione.	I have a cut/a bruise.
Ho una scottatura/una vescica.	I have a burn/a blister.
Ho mal di stomaco/mal d'orecchi.	I have stomachache/earache.
Ho mal di testa/mal di denti.	I have a headache/toothache.

Ho un'indigestione/un colpo di sole.	I have indigestion/sunstroke.
Mi può dare delle aspirine?	Can you give me some aspirin?
Vorrei dei cerotti	I'd like some Band-Aids
una benda (elastica)	(elastic) bandage
una crema solare	suntan lotion
Quante volte al giorno . . . ?	How many times a day . . . ?
. . . devo prenderla	. . . should I take it

Medical notices

AMBULATORIO	OUTPATIENT DEPARTMENT
PRONTO SOCCORSO	FIRST AID, EMERGENCY SERVICE
OSPEDALE	HOSPITAL

si è fatta male/she hurt herself

After lunch Giancarlo and Marisa set off for the ferry, but some miles into the countryside they come across an elderly lady who is lying at the side of the road beside her bicycle. Giancarlo stops the car . . .

Giancarlo: **Ha bisogno di aiuto**, signora?

Signora: Ai! **Mi sono fatta male** alla gamba. **Sono caduta** dalla bicicletta . . . e non posso muovere la gamba. Come mi fa male! Può chiamare mia figlia?

Giancarlo: Mi faccia vedere? (He takes a look) Signora, prima devo chiamare un'ambulanza. Dov'è il telefono più vicino? Ah! C'è una casa lì in fondo—vado a telefonare. Tu, Marisa, rimani qui con la signora.

Marisa: (sits down beside her) Si calmi, signora, Giancarlo ritorna subito. No si preoccupi.

(At the nearby house Giancarlo rings the doorbell)

Giancarlo: Posso usare il suo telefono, per favore?
Signore: Entri pure! Cosa è successo?
Giancarlo: **C'è stato un incidente**. Una signora è caduta della bicicletta e
             si è fatta male. Probabilmente **si è rotta** la gamba . . . (dials)
             . . . Pronto? Mi passi il pronto soccorso, per favore.

Accidents and emergencies

Ha bisogno di aiuto?	Do you need help?
Mi sono fatta male alla gamba	I have hurt my leg
al braccio/alla testa	my arm/my head
Sono caduta dalla bicicletta.	I fell off my bicycle.
Non posso muovere la gamba.	I can't move my leg.
Come mi fa male!	It hurts so much!
Può chiamare mia figlia?	Can you call my daughter?
Mi faccia vedere?	Would you let me see?
Devo chiamare un'ambulanza.	I must call an ambulance.
Dov'è il telefono più vicino?	Where's the nearest telephone?
C'è una casa lì in fondo.	There's a house over there.
Rimani qui.	Stay here. (from *rimanere*)
Si calmi/Non si preoccupi.	Calm yourself/Don't worry.
Posso usare il suo telefono?	Can I use your telephone?
Entri pure!	Come in of course!
Che cosa è successo?	What has happened?
C'è stato un incidente.	There has been an accident.
Probabilmente . . .	Probably . . .
. . . si è rotta la gamba	. . . she has broken her leg
. . . si è rotto il braccio	. . . he has broken his arm
Mi passi il pronto soccorso.	Get me the emergency service.
Lei deve andare in ospedale.	You must go to the hospital.
Chiami un medico!/la polizia!	Call a doctor!/the police!
la patente/l'assicurazione	driver's license/insurance
nome e indirizzo	name and address

the way it works

I don't feel well!

There are various ways in which you can describe your symptoms:

Mi sento male.	I feel ill.
Non mi sento bene.	I don't feel well.
Mi fa male il torace.	My chest is hurting. (lit. it hurts to me the chest)

Note that you do not use the possessive adjective (**mio,** etc.) when talking about parts of your body. **Mi** is an indirect object pronoun (to me). See list below.

Ho mal di testa, etc.	I have a headache, etc.
Ho il raffreddore/la tosse.	I have a cold/a cough.

Note that in Italian you say "I have **the** cold," etc., not "**a**" as in English.

Since when?

Da quanto tempo le fa male?	How long has it been hurting?
Da circa due settimane.	For about two weeks.

Da literally means "since" in this context and is followed by the present tense.

Da quanto tempo si sente così?	How long have you been feeling like this? (lit. since how long do you feel thus?)

The perfect tense (using essere)

Although most Italian verbs form their perfect tense with **avere**, there are some which use **essere**. These verbs are mostly those of movement, such as **andare** (to go). In such cases, the ending of the past participle has to agree with the subject of the verb and changes accordingly. Here is an example of a verb in the past tense formed with **essere**:

sono andato/a	I went	siamo andati/e	we went
sei andato/a	you went (fam)	siete andati/e	you went
è andato/a	he/she, you went (formal)	sono andati/e	they went, you went (formal)

Here is a list of some of the most common verbs which use **essere**, together with their past participles:

andare	(to go)	**andato**	venire	(to come)	**venuto**
arrivare	(to arrive)	**arrivato**	partire	(to leave)	**partito**
entrare	(to enter)	**entrato**	uscire	(to go out)	**uscito**
rimanere	(to remain)	**rimasto**	tornare	(to return)	**tornato**
scendere	(to go down)	**sceso**	cadere	(to fall)	**caduto**

In addition, both **essere** and **stare** (to be) take **essere** in the perfect tense and their past participles are identical: **stato**.

Other verbs for which **essere** is needed in the perfect include all reflexives:

Mi sono dimenticato/a	I forgot	Ci siamo ricordati/e	We remembered
Ti sei alzato/a	You got up	Vi siete lavati/e	You washed
Si è fatto male	He hurt himself	Si sono sentiti/e male	They became sick

Indirect object pronouns

Look at the following phrases:

Mi dà un chilo di mele.	Give (to) me a kilo of apples.
Le presento mia moglie.	I present to you my wife.
Mi passi il pronto soccorso.	Give (to) me the emergency service.
Le prescrivo un antibiotico.	I'll prescribe an antibiotic for you.

In each case the pronoun (**mi**, **le**) is the indirect object and the prepositions "for" or "to" are either expressed or understood.

Here is the full list of indirect object pronouns:

mi	(to/for) me	**ci**	(to/for) us
ti	(to/for) you (fam)	**vi**	(to/for) you
le	(to/for) you/her/it		
gli	(to/for) him/it	**loro**	(to/for) them

Position of object pronouns

Note that both direct and indirect pronouns normally come *before* the verb, except when they occur with an infinitive, in which case they may come *after* it and joined to it. Instances of this are common, occurring especially with combinations of verbs containing parts of the verbs **potere**, **volere**, or **dovere**.

Può darmi la patente?	Can you give me your driver's license?

(Equally correct is: Mi può dare la patente?)

Non **voglio** dargli la patente.	I don't want to give him my license.
Deve darmi la patente.	You must give me your driver's license.

When occurring with a perfect infinitive, the pronoun is added to the infinitive of **avere** or **essere**:

Penso di aver**lo** lasciato . . .	I think I left it . . .
Penso di aver**gli** dato la patente.	I think I gave him my license.

Note that when a pronoun is added to an infinitive, the final **e** is left out.

things to do

5.4 Dove fa male? Can you explain what hurts each of the children?

5.5 The whole family has been under the weather! You consult the pharmacist.
1 Say you aren't feeling well. You have been sick and you have a stomachache.
2 Ask how often you should take the tablets.
3 Your daughter has fallen and hurt her knee (*il ginocchio*). Ask for an elastic bandage.
4 Your son has been stung by an insect. Ask if he can give you anything for insect bites.
5 You'd also like some Band-Aids and some suntan lotion.

5.6 Emergency! Can you report the following incidents to the police?
1 There has been an accident. A boy (*un ragazzo*) has fallen off his bike and has hurt his leg. Call a doctor quickly!
2 Your passport has been stolen. You left it in your room at the hotel yesterday, but today it is no longer there.
3 A lady has been taken ill in the street. Send an ambulance!
4 You have lost your bag. You think you left it on the train.

SPORTS AND WEATHER

che sport fai?/what sport do you play?

Marisa and Giancarlo are sitting having breakfast on the terrace of their friend's house in Elba discussing how to spend the day. Giancarlo is eager to try out his new windsurfer.

Marco: Allora, **cosa facciamo** oggi? Andiamo alla spiaggia?

Giancarlo: Certo. **Fa bel tempo** e voglio provare il mio nuovo surf. Ne potremmo noleggiare uno anche per te, Marisa. Che ne dici?

Marisa: Ma **non so andare con il surf**. Non l'ho mai fatto.

Giancarlo: Puoi imparare. Posso mostrarti come si fa. Non è difficile—e **sai nuotare**, vero?

Marisa: Abbastanza bene . . . Ma **oggi c'è vento** . . . e l'acqua è ghiacciata!

Giancarlo: Non preoccuparti. **Proviamo un po'.**

(They continue talking about sports)

Marco: D'estate che sport fai in Inghilterra, Marisa? Ti piace il tennis?

Marisa: Sì, so giocare a tennis ma preferisco il nuoto. E d'inverno faccio lo sci. Vado a sciare sempre in Scozia con la mia famiglia, ma **fa spesso brutto tempo.**

Marco: Davvero? Perchè non vieni qui in Italia? Ci sono delle piste favolose e in più **c'è anche il sole.**

Giancarlo: Ottima idea! L'anno prossimo andiamo tutti insieme.

A matter of sport . . . (For a list of sports and equipment, see p. 82)

Andiamo alla spiaggia?	Shall we go to the beach?
Voglio provare il mio nuovo surf.	I want to try out my new windsurfer.
Vuoi fare il bagno?	Do you want to have a swim?
Vorrei noleggiare . . .	I'd like to rent . . .
. . . um ombrellone	. . . a beach umbrella
. . . una barca a vela	. . . a sailboat
Che ne dici?	What do you think?
Non so andare con il surf.	I don't know how to windsurf.
Posso mostrarti come si fa.	I can show you how it's done.
Preferisco il nuoto.	I prefer swimming.
Sai nuotare, vero?	You can swim, can't you?
So giocare a tennis/al calcio.	I can play tennis/football.
Si può andare a cavallo?	Can one go riding?
Vado a sciare.	I go skiing.
Mi piace far vela/pescare.	I like sailing/fishing.

. . . and weather

le previsioni del tempo	weather forecast
Che tempo farà domani?	What will the weather be tomorrow?
Fa bel tempo	It's lovely weather
brutto tempo	bad weather
Fa caldo/fa freddo.	It's hot/cold.
C'è il sole.	It's sunny.
Il vento è forte/moderato.	The wind is strong/moderate.
Il mare è calmo/mosso/agitato.	The sea is calm/rough/stormy.
L'acqua è bella/ghiacciata.	The water is lovely/freezing.
la pioggia/la nebbia/la nuvola	rain/fog/cloud
Il cielo è coperto/sereno.	The sky is overcast/clear.
Piove/Nevica.	It's raining/It's snowing.
Ci sono trenta gradi.	It's 30 degrees.

sempre, mai, spesso	always, never, often
Proviamo un po'.	Let's give it a try.
d'estate/d'inverno	in summer/in winter
la primavera/l'autunno	spring/autumn
Davvero?	Really?
Perchè non vieni . . . ?	Why don't you come . . . ?
tutti i giorni/tutti insieme	everyday/all together
in più	moreover

SIGHTSEEING AND LEISURE

Museums and art galleries   You normally pay an entrance fee for museums and galleries, unless you are under 18 or over 60. Museum opening times vary considerably so it is advisable to check at the local **ufficio turistico** or **azienda di soggiorno e turismo**. Most museums are closed on Mondays, and many churches are open only in the mornings.

tante cose da vedere!/so much to see!

Paul has spent a busy morning sightseeing in Venice. He meets with Giulia at a café.

Giulia: Ciao! **Cosa hai visto** stamattina?

Paul: Bè . . . molte cose! Ho preso il vaporetto per Piazza San Marco, **ho visitato** la Basilica, il Campanile e il Palazzo Ducale . . .

Giulia: Che ne pensi? **Ti è piaciuto tutto?**

Paul: **Moltissimo**. Ho visto dei quadri magnifici . . . Ma sono un po' stanco adesso! Vorrei visitare l'Accademia più tardi, dopo pranzo.

Giulia: Che peccato! L'Accademia **è chiusa** il pomeriggio—**chiude all'una**. Ti conviene andare domani mattina.

Paul: Sai **quando apre?**

Giulia: Verso le otto e mezzo o le nove, credo.

Paul: Va bene. Allora questo pomeriggio vorrei visitare la Chiesa dei Frari. Senti, cosa facciamo stasera?

Giulia: Vuoi andare a un concerto? Danno un concerto di musica italiana del diciottesimo secolo. Che ne dici?

Paul: **Mi piacerebbe molto**. Ma ci sono posti per questa sera?

Giulia: Non lo so. Andiamo a vedere dopo pranzo.

Sightseeing

Che cosa c'è da vedere?	What is there to see?
C'è tanto da vedere.	There's so much to see.
Cosa ha (i) visto?	What have you seen?
Ho preso il vaporetto.	I took the motorboat.
Che ne pensi?	What do you think of it?
Ti/Le ha piaciuto tutto?	Did you like it all?
moltissimo	very much indeed
ho visitato/vorrei visitare	I visited/I'd like to visit . . .
ho visto/vorrei vedere	I saw/I'd like to see
la basilica, il campanile	basilica, bell tower
la galleria, il museo	gallery, museum
la chiesa, il duomo	church, cathedral
dei quadri magnifici	some magnificient pictures
una mostra d'arte	an art exhibition
ENTRATA LIBERA	ENTRANCE FREE

Opening hours

È chiuso(a)/è aperto(a).	It is closed/open.
Chiude all'una.	It closes at one.
Lunedì chiuso	Closed on Mondays
A che ora apre?	What time does it open?
Sai quando chiude?	Do you know when it closes?
Ti conviene andare domani.	You'd better go tomorrow.

Plans for the evening

Cosa facciamo stasera?	What will we do this evening?
Vuoi andare . . .	Do you want to go . . .
. . . a un concerto?	. . . to a concert?
. . . al teatro/all'opera . . .	. . . to the theater/the opera?
Danno un concerto.	There is a concert. (lit. they give)
musica del diciottesimo secolo	eighteenth-century music
Mi piacerebbe molto.	I'd like to very much.
Ci sono posti per questa sera?	Are there seats for this evening?
Andiamo a vedere	We'll go and find out
. . . dopo pranzo	. . . after supper

the way it works

Do you know how to . . . ?

Sapere means "to know" or "to know about" something.
Non lo **so**.   I don't know.
Sai quando parte il treno?   Do you know when the train leaves?

Here is the present tense:
so   I know   sappiamo we know
sai   you know (fam)   sapete   you know
sa   he/she knows, you know (formal) sanno   they know, you know (formal)

You also use the verb **sapere** to mean "to know how to" or "to be able to":
Sai far vela?   Do you know how to sail?
Sapete giocare al calcio?   Can you play football?

The weather

Note that the verb **fare** is often used when talking about the weather.
Che tempo **fa?**   What's the weather like?
Fa bel tempo/brutto tempo.   It's nice weather/bad weather.
Fa caldo/freddo.   It's hot/cold.

All and everything

"All" or "everything" in Italian is **tutto/a**:
Tutto bene?   Is everything all right?
Tutto a posto.   Everything's in order.

Note the following expressions using **tutto** in the plural:
tutti i giorni   everyday   **tutti** insieme   all together

things to do

6.1 **Un'inchiesta.** In a survey you are asked to state what sports you play.
     Can you say whether or not you can play the following sports and
     games?
     Sai giocare . . .
     a tennis   al calcio   a rugby   a golf   a scacchi (chess)

     Sai . . .
     nuotare   sciare   pescare   far vela   andare a cavallo (to ride).

6.2 Next question. What do you like doing in your spare time? Can you say whether you enjoy the following activities?
1 Uscire con gli amici
2 Fare dello sport
3 Andare al teatro, al cinema, ai concerti, ecc.
4 Visitare dei musei, delle gallerie, ecc.
5 Viaggiare all'estero (abroad)
6 Rimanere a casa, fare giardinaggio, ecc.
7 Ascoltare (listen to) la radio, guardare la televisione, ecc.

6.3 In Rome you overhear part of a conversation between a local resident and a tourist who is asking for information. Can you figure out what the tourist is asking?

Turista: . . . . ?
Passante: No, il Pantheon è già chiuso.
Turista: . . . . ?
Passante: Chiude alle sedici e mezzo.
Turista: . . . . ?
Passante: Apre alle nove.
Turista: . . . . ?
Passante: No, è chiuso il lunedì.

6.4 Can you match the following questions and answers?

1 Cosa facciamo?	(a) Mi piace, ma preferisco il tennis.
2 Sa nuotare il bambino?	(b) No, piove sempre.
3 Fa bel tempo in Scozia d'inverno?	(c) Andiamo a una partita di calcio.
4 Vuoi fare il bagno?	(d) Sì, nuota come un pesce!
5 Ti piace il golf?	(e) Perchè no? Ottima idea!

6.5 **Tempo Previsto**. What's the weather like?
1 sulle regioni centrali? 2 sulle regioni settentrionali? 3 sulle regioni meridionali?

ENTERTAINMENT

Theater, concerts   Throughout the year there are many opera, music, and drama festivals in Italy. In Venice the most important festival is the **Biennale**, while in Florence there is a big music festival, **Maggio Musicale**, in May and June. There are opera houses in Milan, Rome, Venice, Florence, and Naples, and operas are also performed in many other Italian towns.

nel ufficio prenotazioni/at the ticket office

In Florence, Raffaella is trying to buy tickets for the opera *La Traviata*.

Raffaella:	Buongiorno. **Vorrei prenotare due posti** per lo spettacolo di martedì dodici giugno.
Impiegato:	Mi dispiace, signora, non abbiamo più posti per quella sera. È tutto esaurito.
Raffaella:	Peccato! Allora, **ci sono posti per venerdì?**
Impiegato:	Venerdì quindici giugno. Vediamo . . . Sì, sì, per venerdì ci sono posti in galleria e alcune poltrone.
Raffaella:	Quanto costano i posti in galleria?
Impiegato:	In galleria costano trentamila lire.
Raffaella:	**Mi dà due biglietti** in galleria, per favore.
Impiegato:	Va bene, signora.
Raffaella:	**A che ora incomincia** lo spettacolo?
Impiegato:	Alle nove.

Buying tickets

Vorrei due Biglietti per . . .	I'd like two tickets for . . .
lo spettacolo/il concerto	the performance/the concert
martedì dodici giugno	Tuesday June 12
Non abbiamo più posti.	We have no seats left.
È tutto esaurito.	It's completely full.
Ci sono posti?	Are there any seats?
un posto in galleria/una poltrona	balcony seat/seat
alcune poltrone	a few seats
A che ora incomincia . . .?	What time does . . . begin?
FERIALI/FESTIVI	WEEKDAYS/PUBLIC HOLIDAYS

Cinema   Look at the entertainment page of the local newspaper or an entertainment guide to discover what's happening. Films which have not been dubbed into Italian will be advertised as being in the original language (**in lingua originale** or **versione originale**) with subtitles (**sottotitoli**).

Il programma degli spettacoli/the entertainment page

Giancarlo and Marisa are thinking about going to the cinema, but they discover they have different tastes . . .

Marisa: Io vorrei vedere un film. Che cosa danno?

Giancarlo: **Niente di interessante**—un western. **Non mi piacciono molto** gli western.

Marisa: Ma a me piacciono moltissimo! Come si chiama?

Giancarlo: È un film vecchio che ho già visto due volte. Si chiama *Il bello, il brutto e il cattivo.*

Marisa: È un classico, e io non l'ho mai visto. Per favore, Giancarlo, **mi piacerebbe molto** vederlo.

Giancarlo: Va bene—andiamo. La settimana scorsa ho visto *Stregata dalla luna* con Cher che mi è piaciuto molto. In generale **mi piacciono di più** i film gialli e le commedie. Ma non importa. Facciamo i biglietti adesso e mangiamo dopo aver visto il film. **Conosco una trattoria buonissima** vicino al cinema.

Giving your opinion

niente di interessante	nothing interesting
un film vecchio . . .	an old film . . .
. . . che ho già visto	. . . which I have already seen
due volte	twice
un classico	a classic
Io non l'ho mai visto.	I have never seen it.
Mi piacerebbe molto vederlo.	I'd love to see it.
a me piace di più	I prefer
i film gialli	thrillers
le commedie	comedies
Regia di . . .	Directed by . . .
Facciamo i biglietti.	We'll buy the tickets.
Mangiamo dopo aver visto il film.	We'll eat after having seen the film.
Conosco una trattoria buonissima.	I know an excellent restaurant.
INGRESSO L4000/RIDOTTO L2000	ENTRANCE FEE/REDUCED

the way it works

Negatives

Look at the following phrases:

Non abbiamo **più** posti.   We have no seats left. (lit. no longer)
Non vede **nessuno.**   He sees nobody.
Non danno **niente** d'interessante.   They are showing nothing interesting.
Non l'ho **mai** visto.   I have never seen it.
Non l'ho **ancora** fatto.   I haven't done it yet.

Before and after

"Beforehand," "first" is **prima**. "Before . . . " is **prima di**:
prima delle nove   before 9 o'clock
Ceniamo **prima di** partire.   We'll have supper before we go.

"Afterward," "later" is **dopo**. "After . . . " is also **dopo**:
Dopo le sette   after 7 o'clock
Ceniamo **dopo** aver visto il film.   We'll have supper after having seen the film.

Dates

Dates are always given in cardinal numbers (see p. 78), except for the first of the month:

il primo luglio   the first of July
il diciassette agosto   the seventeenth of August
il ventinove dicembre   the twenty-ninth of December

Here are some other useful expressions with days of the week and dates:

Chiuso il lunedì   Closed on Monday(s)
tutti i sabato   Every Saturday
venerdì trenta luglio   Friday July 30
Nel novantadue   In 1992

Future intentions

Italian often uses the present tense where English needs a future tense, to express intention or suggestion. There are some instances of this in this unit:

Facciamo i biglietti.   We'll buy the tickets.
Mangiamo dopo.   We'll eat afterwards.

To know a person or a place

While **sapere** means to know *about something,* if you want to say that you know *a person or a place,* you use the verb **conoscere**:

Conosci Pietro?   Do you know Peter?
Non conosco Venezia.   I don't know Venice.
Conosco una trattoria.   I know a restaurant.

things to do

6.6 You are at the box office trying to buy tickets for a play.

You:	[Say you want four tickets for the performance on Wednesday May 19]
Impiegato:	Mi dispiace, per mercoledì no abbiamo più posti.
You:	[Ask if there are any tickets for Thursday]
Impiegato:	Sì, abbiamo alcuni posti in galleria.
You:	[Ask how much they are]
Impiegato:	Diciassettemila lire.
You:	[Say you'd like four tickets and ask how much it comes to]

6.7
1 What is being advertised here?
2 Who is the author?
3 Who is the director?
4 When and at what time is it being broadcast?
5 What is RaiDue?

TEATRO D'ESTATE
Paolo Stoppa
in
IL BERRETTO A SONAGLI
di Luigi Pirandello
DOMANI SERA ALLE 22
RAIDUE
Regia di
Luigi Squarzina

6 Can you guess what play this is?

DA VENERDI' TUTTE LE SERE
TEATRO E CINEMA GIALLO
Ore 20: PRIMO FILM GIALLO

Ore 21,15
TRAPPOLA PER TOPI

Commedia in due atti

di **AGATHA CHRISTIE**
con **ENZA GIOVINE**
*Il giallo che da 35 anni
trionfa a Londra*

6.8
1 What is being advertised?
2 When is it on?
3 Which day is it not open?
4 How much does it cost?

**MUSEO D'ARTE CONTEMPORANEA
– CASTELLO DI RIVOLI:** mostra
Joan Mirò. Viaggio delle figure, 4
giugno-18 settembre; collezione.
Aperto da martedì a domenica ore
10–19, lunedì chiuso. Ingresso L.
4000, ridotto L. 2000. Per informazioni tel. 958.15.47.

TALKING ABOUT YOURSELF

sono insegnante/I'm a teacher

Marisa hopes that she will be offered a job as a teacher of English and won't have to return to England. Marco is asking her about what she was doing before she came to Italy.

Marco: Che cosa fai, Marisa?

Marisa: **Sono insegnante. Insegnavo l'inglese** in una scuola di lingue a Londra.

Marco: Ti piaceva? Com'è la vita a Londra?

Marisa: **Abitavo** in un appartamento con mia sorella. La mattina prendevo la metropolitana per andare a scuola— c'era una stazione a due passi dalla scuola, e **lavoravo** dalle nove alle cinque. La sera **uscivo** con gli amici . . . si andava a un *pub* . . . o al teatro, al cinema. Ci sono tante cose interessanti da fare a Londra. Mi divertivo ma . . . **volevo** sempre viaggiare, vedere il mondo.

Marco: Dunque adesso vai a insegnare a Firenze?
Marisa: Lo spero proprio! Domani torniamo a Firenze e spero di
          cominciare a lavorare subito.
Marco: Mi piacerebbe imparare l'inglese. Vorresti insegnare anche a
          me?
Marisa: Con piacere! Ma ti avverto, sono molto severa!

Your work (For a list of professions, see p. 79)

Sono insegnante.	I'm a teacher.
Insegnavo l'inglese.	I was teaching English.
Prendeva la metropolitana.	I went by subway.
per andare a scuola	to go to the school
c'era una stazione	there was a station
a due passi dalla scuola	very close to the school
Lavoravo dalle nove alle cinque.	I was working from 9 till 5.
Vai a insegnare a Firenze.	You are going to teach in Florence.
Lo spero proprio.	I hope so very much.
Spero di cominciare a lavorare subito.	I'm hoping to start work at once.
Mi piacerebbe imparare l'inglese.	I'd like to learn English.
Vorresti insegnare anche a me?	Would you teach me too?
Con piacere!	With pleasure!
Ma ti avverto, sono molto severa!	I warn you, I'm very strict!

After work

Uscivo con gli amici.	I used to go out with friends.
Si andava a un *pub,* al teatro.	We would go to a pub, to the theater.
Mi divertivo . . .	I was enjoying myself . . .
Ero più felice che a Roma.	I was happier than in Rome.
Volevo sempre viaggiare.	I always wanted to travel.
vedere il mondo	to see the world

che lavoro fa?/what's your job?

Raffaella is stopped in the street by a reporter who asks her some questions . . .

Intervistatore: Scusi, signora, sto facendo un'inchiesta per la RAI sugli
                  abitanti di Firenze e il loro lavoro. Vorrei farle alcune
                  domande.
Raffaella: Con piacere.
Intervistatore: Come si chiama, per favore?
Raffaella: Raffaella Festoso.
Intervistatore: **Quanti anni ha?**
Raffaella: Trentadue.
Intervistatore: **Di dov'è lei?** Di Firenze?
Raffaella: No, **sono nata a Roma.**
Intervistatore: Perchè è venuta qui?
Raffaella: Per studiare. Studiavo qui all'università di Firenze e mi
                  piaceva stare qui. Ero più felice che a Roma. Dopo gli studi
                  universitari ho trovato un posto qui.

Intervistatore:	Che lavora fa?
Raffaella:	**Faccio la disegnatrice** di moda. Lavoro per una ditta di tessuti.
Intervistatore:	È sposata?
Raffaella:	Sì. **Mio marito è medico**. Ci siamo incontrati dieci anni fa mentre eravamo studenti.
Intervistatore:	Dunque, lavorate tutti i due?
Raffaella:	Sì, ma io lavoro solamente la mattina.
Intervistatore:	Ha figli?
Raffaella:	Sì, abbiamo un figlio e una figlia. **Il bambino ha otto anni** e la bambina cinque.
Intervistatore:	Dove abitate?
Raffaella:	Abitiamo in un vecchio appartamento al centro.
Intervistatore:	Grazie.
Raffaella:	Prego. Buongiorno.

Faccio la disegnatrice.	I work as a designer.
Lavoro per una ditta di tessuti.	I work for a fabric company.
È medico.	He's a doctor.
Faceva medicina.	He was studying medicine.
Lavorate tutti i due?	Do you both work?
Lavoro solamente la mattina.	I work mornings only.
Quanto guadagna?	How much do you earn?
Non guadagno molto.	I don't earn much.

Your home

Sono nata a Roma.	I was born in Rome.
Sono venuta qui per studiare.	I came here to study.
Ci siamo incontrati dieci anni fa.	We met ten years ago.
mentre eravamo studenti	when we were students
Dove abitate?	Where do you live?
Abitiamo in un appartamento.	We live in an apartment.
Abitavo in un appartamento	I was living in an apartment
. . . in una casa	. . . in a house
. . . in una villetta	. . . a small house
le stanze, le camere	the rooms
camere da letto, bagno	bedrooms, bathroom
sala da pranzo, cucina	dining room, kitchen
soggiorno, sala	living room
giardino, terrazzo/balcone	garden, terrace/balcony

Your status

È sposato/a?	Are you married?
Sì, sono sposato/a.	Yes, I'm married.
fidanzato/a, vedovo/a	engaged/widow(er)
Ha figli?	Do you have any children?
Abbiamo un figlio e una figlia.	We have a son and a daughter.

Your age

Quanti anni ha?	How old are you?
trentadue	thirty-two
Il bambino ha otto anni.	The boy is eight.
la bambina cinque	the girl five

the way it works

Imperfect tense

Look at the following examples from the dialogue:

Abita**vo** in un appartamento.	I was living in an apartment. (= used to)
Insegna**vo** l'inglese.	I was teaching English.
Prendevo la metropolitana.	I took the subway. (= habitual action)
Usci**vo** con gli amici.	I went out with friends.

To talk about what you used to do or the way things used to be, you use the imperfect tense. It is formed like this:
From the infinitive of the verb (e.g., **abitare, prendere, uscire**) take away the **-re** and add the following endings:

abitare	abita	**-vo**	I lived	volere	vole	**-vamo**	we wanted
insegnare	insegna	**-vi**	you taught	uscire	usci	**-vate**	you went out
prendere	prende	**-va**	he/you took	venire	veni	**-vano**	they, you came

Most verbs conform to this pattern. One exception, however, is **essere**.

ero	I was	eravamo	we were
eri	you were (familiar)	eravate	you were
era	he/she/it was, you were (formal)	erano	they were, you were (formal)

A few other verbs use a slightly different stem: for example, **fare**.

facevo	I was doing, making, etc.	facevamo	we were doing
facevi	you were doing	facevate	you were doing
faceva	he/she/it/you were doing	facevano	they/you were doing

This tense is frequently used to express what was going on when something happened:
Ci sono incontrati mentre **eravamo** studenti. We met each other when were students.

Sto facendo un'inchiesta

If you want to emphasize the present time of an action, you can use the present tense of **stare** (see p. 11) + a form of the verb called the present participle.
The present participle is formed as follows:
-are verbs: remove **-are** and add **-ando**.
sto parl**ando** I am talking; **sta** pens**ando** he is thinking
-ere and **-ire** verbs: remove **-ere/-ire** and add **-endo**.

Cosa state fac**endo**?	What are you doing?
Stiamo usc**endo**.	We are going out.

Adverbs

Adverbs are usually formed in Italian by adding **-mente** to the adjective. Adjectives which end in **-o** form their adverb from the feminine form (= **a**):

lento/lenta   lentamente (slowly)   vero/vera   veramente (truly)

Adjectives ending in **-e** simply add **-mente**. But those ending in **-le** or **-re** drop the final **-e**:

facile   facilmente   difficile   difficilmente

things to do

7.1 Che lavoro fa? Your friends are talking about what they do. Can you answer for them? Use **Sono** . . . or **Faccio il/la** . . .

Pietro	[doctor]	Marco	[architect]
Raffaella	[designer]	Paul	[company director]
Marisa	[teacher]	Giulia	[music student]
Giancarlo	[accountant]	You	(*see list of jobs, p. 79*)

7.2 You have gotten into conversation with the owner of a small factory **(una azienda)** making leather goods, and you would like to know more about him:

You:	[Ask him how long he has had the factory]
Signore:	Da circa venti anni.
You:	[Ask him where he learned to do this work]
Signore:	Da ragazzo, ho imparato qui in bottega.
You:	[You want to know how many people work here]
Signore:	Adesso nella bottega ci sono quattro persone.
You:	[Thank him very much]

7.3 Now it's your turn to be interviewed. The owner of the hotel where you're staying wants to know about your childhood . . .

Signora:	Di dov'è lei?
You:	[Say you were born in the United States]
Signora:	Da ragazzo, dove abitava? In campagna o in città?
You:	[Say you lived in a village **(un paese)** in a small house, with a garden]
Signora:	Quanti eravate in famiglia? Aveva fratelli o sorelle?
You:	[Say you have a brother and a sister]
Signora:	I suoi genitori vivono ancora?
You:	[Say your mother is still alive. She is now a widow of seventy-six]
Signora:	E suo fratello?
You:	[Say he is married with two children. He's a painter]
Signora:	E sua sorella?
You:	[Say she's not married. She's an accountant and works in Chicago]

MAKING CONVERSATION

Camping There are over 1,600 campsites in Italy and camping is very popular. Tourist offices have lists of local sites and their facilities. The Touring Club Italiano publishes full details of all the authorized sites in *Campeggi e Villaggi Turistici in Italia* (TCI, Corso Italia 10, Milano). Fees vary according to the area and type of site.

da quanto tempo è qui?/how long have you been here?

Back in Florence, Giulia has invited some of her friends to meet Paul on his last evening in Italy. A friend called Franco is asking Paul about his week.

Franco: **Da quanto tempo è qui** in Italia?
Paul: **Da soltanto una settimana.**
Franco: È venuto qui per lavoro o in vacanza?
Paul: Sono venuto qui per lavoro ma sono riuscito a visitare anche Venezia, che **non avevo mai visto**.
Franco: Allora, qual'è la città che le è piaciuta di più?
Paul: Bè . . . È difficile. Non lo so. Conosco Firenze meglio, ma tutte e due sono bellissime. Che ne pensa lei?

Franco: Io sono di Napoli e preferisco il sud di Italia—**è più** selvaggio del nord e **c'è meno** gente. Senti, Giulia, andiamo al sud per le vacanze?

Giulia: Forse. Ma ti ricordi l'anno scorso, quando siamo andati in campeggio con la tua macchina vecchia? Che disastro! (turns to Paul) Siamo andati a fare campeggio in montagna. Prima di tutto, abbiamo avuto un guasto in autostrada. Poi, arrivati finalmente al campeggio che cercavamo, lo abbiamo trovato completo.

Franco: Sì, mi ricordo. Abbiamo trovato un altro campeggio più tardi e dopo aver messo la tenda, avevamo fame. Ma . . . **avevamo dimenticato** di portare il fornello a gas . . .!

Giulia: Che catastrofe! Ma quest'anno hai una macchina nuova e non dimentichiamo niente!

Small talk

per lavoro/in vacanza	on business/on vacation
Qual'è la città che . . .	Which city . . .
. . . le è piaciuta di più?	. . . did you like more?
Conosco Firenze meglio.	I know Florence better.
Sono riuscito a visitare Venezia.	I managed to visit Venice.
Tutte e due sono bellissime.	Both (cities) are lovely.
È più selvaggio del nord.	It's wilder than the north.
C'è meno gente.	There are fewer people.

Telling a story

Siamo andati a fare campeggio.	We went camping.
in montagna	in the mountains
Abbiamo avuto un guasto.	We had a breakdown.
arrivati al campeggio	when we arrived at the campsite
. . . che cercavamo	. . . which we were looking for
lo abbiamo trovato completo	we found it was full
dopo aver messo la tenda	after having put up the tent
avevamo fame	we were hungry
avevamo dimenticato di . . .	we had forgotten to
portare il fornello a gas	bring the gas stove

Camping language

C'è un campeggio qui vicino?	Is there a campsite near here?
C'è posto per una tenda/una roulotte?	Is there room for a tent/trailer?
l'acqua potabile/l'elettricità	drinking water/electricity
una piscina/dei negozi	swimming pool/stores
Dove sono i gabinetti/le docce?	Where are the toilets/showers?

USEFUL WORDS AND PHRASES

Non dimentichiamo niente!	We won't forget anything!
Che disastro!/Che catastrofe!	How awful!
forse	perhaps

SAYING GOODBYE

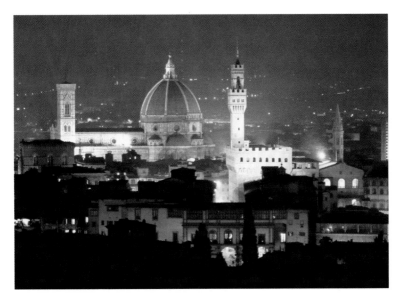

grazie e arrivederci/thank you and goodbye

At the end of the evening, Paul is saying his farewells.

Giulia: **Prendi un'altra birra?**

Paul: **No, grazie, basta così. Me ne devo andare. Parto domani mattina** presto e non ho ancora fatto la valigia. Devo essere all'aeroporto di Pisa alle dieci.

Giulia: Che peccato! **Quando ritorni** a Firenze?

Paul: L'anno prossimo, spero—in primavera. Mi auguro che tutto vada bene con gli esami. Dopo le vacanze **perchè non vieni in Inghilterra?**

Giulia: Buona idea! **Mi puoi dare il tuo indirizzo?**

Paul: Certo . . . Eccolo. Allora, grazie e arrivederci.

Giulia: Arrivederci.

The end of the party

Prendi un'altra birra?	Have another beer?
No, grazie, basta così.	No, thanks. I've had enough.
Me ne devo andare.	I must go.
Parto domani presto.	I'm leaving tomorrow early.
Non ho ancora fatto la valigia.	I haven't yet packed my suitcase.
Devo essere all'aeroporto.	I must be at the airport.
l'anno prossimo in primavera	next year in the spring
Quando ritorni?	When are you coming back?
Mi auguro che tutto vada bene.	I hope all goes well.
con gli esami	with the exams
Perchè non vieni in Inghilterra?	Why don't you come to England?
Mi puoi dare il tuo indirizzo?	Can you give me your address?

the way it works

More or less

"More" is **più**. "More . . . than" is **più . . . che** or **de**. "Less" or "fewer" is **meno**.

Ero **più** felice **che** a Roma.	I was happier than in Rome.
. . . è **più** selvaggio **del** nord	. . . it's wilder than the north
C'è **meno** gente.	There are fewer people.

Note that **di più** means "most":

Che le è piaciuta di più?	Which did you like most?

Note: although **più** and **meno** can be used with most comparatives, there are some which require more specialized words:

buono (good)	migliore (better)	malo (bad)	peggiore (worse) (adjective)
bene (good)	meglio (better)	male (bad)	peggio (worse) (adverb)

Imperfect of avere

avevo una sorella	I had a sister
avevamo fame	we were hungry

The formation of the imperfect of **avere** is as follows:

avevo	I had	avevamo	we had
avevi	you had (familiar)	avevate	you had
aveva	he/she had, you had (formal)	avevano	they had, you had (formal)

Pluperfect tense

To say what you had done or describe what had happened, you need to use the pluperfect tense. This is formed with the *imperfect* tense of **avere** (or **essere** if the verb takes **essere** in the perfect) + the past participle:

. . . che non **avevo** mai visto	. . . which I hadn't seen before . . .
. . . **avevamo** dimenticato di . . .	. . . we had forgotten to . . .

things to do

7.4 Bigger and better! The children are making comparisons—to their advantage, naturally! (NB Review possessives on p. 5.)

1 La mia casa è molto grande!   [But mine is bigger than yours!]

2 La mia macchina è nuova . . .

3 . . . È anche molto veloce.

4 Mio fratello è alto.

5 I nostri gelati sono buonissimi!

7.5 Things weren't exactly as you expected! Can you relate in Italian the following mishaps?

1 When you arrived at the cathedral, you found it was shut.

2 After having put up the tent, you wanted to go to bed (**andare a letto**), but you found you had forgotten your sleeping bag (**il sacco a pelo**).

3 You looked for (**cercare** = to look for) your suitcase but you had left it in the train.

4 You arrived at the station but the train had already gone.

7.6 You are chatting with the owner of a local café who is interested in you and your family.

Amico: Perche è venuto qui . . . in vacanza or per lavoro?

You: [Say you came on vacation]

Amico: È venuto da solo?

You: [No, say you came with your wife and daughter]

Amico: Quanti anni ha la bambina?

You: [She's ten]

Amico: Dove siete andati?

You: [Say you went camping in Tuscany]

Amico: Vi è piaciuta, la Toscana?

You: [Yes, say you liked it very much, there are some lovely old towns and the countryside (**la campagna**) is fabulous]

Amico: Siete andati a Siena?

You: [Say yes, you stopped off there for lunch one day. There is a lot to see—it's very interesting. Ask him if he knows it]

Amico: Sì, molto bene. Sono nato lì—è il mio paese nativo.

You: [It's very beautiful]

Amico: Faceva bel tempo, vero?

You: [Yes, it was hot and sunny every day until yesterday (**fino a ieri**) when there was a storm]

Amico: E dove andate adesso?

You: [Say unfortunately you have to go home tomorrow. You have to be at the airport by noon]

1.1 1 Buongiorno, signore. 2 Buongiorno, signora. 3 Ciao, Claudia. 4 Buonasera, signori. 5. Buonsera, signorina. 6 Ciao, Mauro.

1.2 1 (Mi chiamo) Henry Jones./Sì, sono Susan Jones. 2 (Mi chiamo) Patricia Fox./Si chiama Ben.

1.3 1(c). 2(a). 3(d). 4(e). 5(b).

1.4 1 una doppia con bagno. 2 una singola con doccia. 3 una doppia con due letti. 4 una singola con vista sul mare. 5 due camere singole con bagno.

1.5 1 Sono le tre. 2 Sono le tre e cinque. 3 Sono le tre e venti. 4 Sono le tre meno quarto. 5 È l'una.

1.6 Due birre/Tre bicchieri di vino rosso/ Un tè al limone/Un caffè.

2.1 1 Scusi, dov'è la Piazza della Repubblica? 2 Scusi, dov'è il Palazzo Vecchio? 3 Scusi, dov'è la Galleria degli Uffizi? 4 Scusi, dov'è L'Azienda di Turismo? 5 Scusi, dov'è la posta?

2.2 1 Il Palazzo Vecchio. 2 La Posta. 3 La Piazza della Repubblica. 4 L'Azienda di Turismo.

2.3 1(c). 2(d). 3(e). 4(b). 5(a).

2.4 Vorrei un vestito rosso; vorrei una gonna verde; vorrei dei pantaloni blu.

2.5 1 Mi piace quest'anello. Quanto costa? 2 Mi piace questo profumo. Quanto costa? 3 Mi piacciono queste cinture. Quanto costano? 4 Mi piace questa macchina fotografica. Quanto costa? 5 Mi piacciono queste cassette. Quanto costano?

2.6 . . . un paio di . . ./Numero trentanove/non mi piace il colore/Posso provarli?/Sono troppo stretti/Sì, grazie/ Questi . . ./ . . .buongiorno.

3.1 del pane casereccio; delle mele e pere; dell'uva bianca; dei pomodori; del maiale; del prosciutto; degli spaghetti; del formaggio; dell'olio; dello zucchero.

3.2 due etti di burro; un litro di latte; una bottiglia di vino rosso; mezzo chilo di caffè; un chilo di spaghetti; due chili di mele rosse; un chilo e mezzo di pomodori maturi.

3.3 quattrocento (4 postcards); novecento (2 stamps); millecinquecento (English newspaper); seimilaseicento (2 boxes of chocolates).

3.4 1 Mi porti un'altra sedia, per piacere? 2 Mi porti il sale e il pepe, per favore? 3 Avete pollo arrosto? 4 Avete patate fritte?

3.5 Siamo tre. Ha un tavolo sulla terrazza?/Sì, va bene/Per la signora, zuppa di pesce e una cotoletta al marsala. Per il signore, tagliatelle alle vongole e una bistecca alla griglia. Per me, cannelloni al forno e petti di pollo./Ci può portare degli zucchini, dei funghi, e dei fagiolini/Una bottiglia di Orvieto e mezzo litro di acqua minerale.

4.1 Buongiorno. Vorrei cambiare cinquanta sterline./Sì, eccolo. Quant'è il cambio?/No, mi dia (dà) due biglietti da cinquantamila.

4.2 A che ora parte il treno per Siena?/È diretto o devo cambiare?/A che ora arriva a Siena?/Quanto costa il biglietto?/Andata e ritorno.

4.3 *Bologna:* il treno parte alle nove e quindici e arriva alle undice e quarantacinque. *Torino:* Parte alle dieci e venti e arriva alle dodici e cinquanta. *Firenze:* Parte alle undici e trenta e arriva alle quindici e trenta. *Ancona:* Parte alle dodici e due e arriva alle diciotto. *Roma:* Parte alle tredici e quaranta e arriva alle ventuno e trenta.

4.4 Carla va in Inghilterra. Va in aereo./ Leo va in Francia. Va in macchina./Antonio va a Napoli. Va in treno./Giulia va a Orvieto. Va in pullman.

4.5 C'è un pullman per Milano?/Quando parte il prossimo pullman per Milano?/ Quanto tempo ci impiega?/Quanto costa il biglietto?/Andata./Va bene. Mi dà una andata.

4.6 1 Prenda la prima strada sulla destra. È sulla sinistra. 2 Vada fino al semaforo e attraversi la strada. È proprio lì, sulla destra.

5.1 1 Vorrei la benzina senza piombo. 2 Trenta litri, per favore. 3 Mi può controllare l'olio, per favore? 4 Grazie. Quant'è?

5.2 1 No Entry. 2 No Parking. 3 No Passing.

5.3 Mi dispiace. Credo di aver lasciato la mia macchina fotografica qui/L'ho messa sulla tavola in fondo. Ho comprato una bibita e poi ho dimenticato di prenderla./Ah sì, questa è la mia. Grazie mille, signora.

5.4 1 Ha mal di stomaco. 2 Le fa male il ginocchio. 3 Gli fa male il dito.

5.5 1 Non mi sento bene. Ho vomitato e ho mal di stomaco. 2 Quante volte al giorno devo prendere le compresse? 3 Mia figlia è caduta e si è fatta male al ginocchio. Ha una benda elastica? 4 Mio figlio è stato punto. Ha qualcosa per le punture d'insetto? 5 Anche vorrei dei cerotti e della crema solare.

5.6 1 C'è stato un incidente. Un ragazzo è caduto dalla bicicletta e si è fatto male alla gamba. Chiami un medico presto! 2 Mi è stato rubato il passaporto. L'ho lasciato ieri nella camera dell'albergo ma oggi non c'è più. 3 Una signora si è sentita male nella strada. Chiami un'ambulanza! 4 Ho perso la mia borsa. Credo di averla lasciata nel treno.

6.1 So (Non so) giocare a tennis, giocare a calcio, giocare a rugby, giocare a golf, giocare a scacchi. So (Non so) nuotare, sciare, pescare, far vela, andare a cavallo.

6.2 Mi piace/Non mi piace . . .

6.3 Il Pantheon è aperto?/A che ora chiude?/A che ora apre?/È aperto tutti i giorni?

6.4 1(c). 2(d). 3(b). 4(e). 5(a).

6.5 1 Piove. Fa brutto tempo. 2 Nevica. Fa freddo. 3 C'è il sole. Fa molto caldo.

6.6 Vorrei quattro biglietti per lo spettacolo di mercoledì diciannove maggio./Ci sono posti per giovedì?/Quanto costano?/Allora quattro biglietti, per favore.

6.7 1 A play. 2 Luigi Pirandello. 3 Luigi Squarzina. 4 Sunday evening at 10 p.m. 5 Channel 2. 6 *The Mousetrap.*

6.8 1 An exhibition of works by Mirò 2

June 4 to September 18. 3 Monday. 4 4,000 lire (reduced price 2,000 lire).

7.1 Sono medico; disegnatrice; insegnante; ragioniere; architetto; direttore; studente di musica.

7.2 Da quanto tempo ha questa azienda?/Dove ha imparato a fare questo lavoro?/Quante persone lavorano qui?/Molte grazie.

7.3 Sono nato/a nel sud dell'Inghilterra./Abitavamo in una villetta, una villetta con giardino, in un paese./Ho un fratello e una sorella./Mia madre vive ancora. È vedova e ha settantasei anni./Mio fratello è sposato e ha due bambini. È pittore./Mia sorella non è sposata. Lavora a Londra—è ragioniera.

7.4 1 La mia è più grande! 2 La mia è più nuova. 3 Anche è più veloce. 4 Mio fratello è più alto. 5 I nostri gelati sono migliori.

7.5 1 Arrivato al duomo, lo avevo trovato chiuso. 2 Dopo aver messo la tenda, volevo andare a letto, ma avevo dimenticato di portare il sacco a pelo. 3 Ho cercato la mia valigia, ma l'avevo lasciata nel treno. 4 Sono arrivato alla stazione ma il treno era partito.

7.6 Sono venuto qui in vacanza./No, sono venuto con mia moglie e mia figlia./Ha dieci anni./Siamo andati in campeggio in Toscana./Sì, ci ha piaciuta molto la Toscana. Ci sono delle vecchie città bellissime e la campagna è favolosa./Sì, ci siamo fermati un giorno per pranzare. C'è tanto da vedere—molte cose interessanti. La conosce lei?/È bellissima./Sì, faceva bel tempo tutti i giorni fino a ieri. Ieri c'era una tempesta./Sfortunatamente domani dobbiamo andare a casa. Dobbiamo essere all'aeroporto a mezzogiorno.

VOCABULARY

English–Italian topic vocabularies

Numbers 0–100

0	zero	11	undici	21	ventuno	40	quaranta
1	uno	12	dodici	22	ventidue	50	cinquanta
2	due	13	tredici	23	ventitrè	60	sessanta
3	tre	14	quattordici	24	ventiquattro	70	settanta
4	quattro	15	quindici	25	venticinque	80	ottanta
5	cinque	16	sedici	26	ventisei	90	novanta
6	sei	17	diciassette	27	ventisette	100	cento
7	sette	18	diciotto	28	ventotto		
8	otto	19	diciannove	29	ventinove		
9	nove	20	venti	30	trenta		
10	dieci						

Numbers 101–100,000

101	centouno	2,000	duemila
102	centodue	3,000	tremila
110	cento dieci	4,000	quattromila
200	duecento	5,000	cinquemila
300	trecento	6,000	seimila
400	quattrocento		
500	cinquecento	10,000	diecimila
600	seicento	20,000	ventimila
700	settecento	30,000	cinquantamila
800	ottocento	100,000	centomila
900	novecento	500,000	cinquecentomila
1000	mille	1,000,000	un milione

Ordinal numbers

first	primo/a
second	secondo/a
third	terzo/a
fourth	quarto/a
fifth	quinto/a
sixth	sesto/a
seventh	settimo/a
eighth	ottavo/a
ninth	nono/a
tenth	decimo/a

Months

January	gennaio
February	febbraio
March	marzo
April	aprile
May	maggio
June	giugno
July	luglio
August	agosto
September	settembre
October	ottobre
November	novembre
December	dicembre

VOCABULARY

Days of the week

Monday	lunedì
Tuesday	martedì
Wednesday	mercoledì
Thursday	giovedì
Friday	venerdì
Saturday	sabato
Sunday	domenica
week	la settimana
weekend	il finesettimana
next week	la prossima settimana

Times of the day, etc.

morning	la mattina
afternoon	il pomeriggio
evening	la sera
night	la notte
today	oggi
this morning	stamattina
tomorrow	domani
tomorrow morning	domani mattina
yesterday	ieri
last week	la settimana scorsa

Professions

accountant	ragioniere, ragioniera
architect	architetto
businessman	uomo d'affari
civil servant	funzionario/funzionaria
clerk	impiegato, impiegata
computer operator	operatore
computer programmer	programmatore
dentist	dentista
designer	disegnatore, disegnatrice
doctor	medico
electrician	elettricista
engineer	ingegnere
estate agent	agente immobiliare
journalist	giornalista
lawyer	avvocato
manager, director	direttore
mechanic	meccanico
nurse	infermiere/infermiera
painter	pittore
pensioner	pensionato/pensionata
police officer	poliziotto
potter	ceramista
salesperson	rappresentante
secretary	segretaria
shop assistant	commesso, commessa
student	studente
teacher	insegnante, professore
technician	tecnico
worker, blue-collar worker	operaio

Clothes (l'abbigliamento), etc.

women's/men's	per donna/uomo
children's	per bambini
bikini	il bikini
blouse	la camicetta
bra	il reggiseno
briefs	lo slip
coat	il cappotto
dress	il vestito
gloves	i guanti
handbag, purse	la borsa
handkerchief	il fazzoletto
hat	il cappello
jacket	la giacca
jeans	i jeans
jersey	la maglia
pants	i pantaloni
panty hose	il collant
pullover	il pullover
raincoat	l'impermeabile
scarf	la sciarpa
shirt	la camicia
shorts	i pantaloncini
skirt	la gonna
socks	i calzini
suit (man's)	il completo
suit (woman's)	il tailleur
sweater	il maglione
swimming trunks	i calzoncini da bagno
swimsuit	il costume da bagno
tee-shirt	la maglietta di cotone
tie	la cravatta
tracksuit	la tuta sportiva
tweed jacket and pants	uno spezzato
windbreaker	la giacca a vento

VOCABULARY

Shoes

shoes	le scarpe
boots	gli stivali
clogs	gli zoccoli
sandals	i sandali

Colors

black	nero/a
blue	blu, azzurro/a
brown	marrone
gray	grigio/a
green	verde
orange	arancio/a
pink	rosa
purple	viola
red	rosso/a
white	bianco/a
yellow	giallo/a
light . . .	. . . chiaro/a
dark . . .	. . . scuro/a

Stores (i negozi) and services (i servizi)

bank	la banca
barber's	il barbiere
bookshop	la libreria
camping equipment	il materiale da campeggio
clothing store	l'abbigliamento
dry cleaner's	la lavanderia a secco
hair stylist	il parrucchiere
hardware store	il negozio di ferramenta
jeweler's	la gioielleria
laundromat	la lavanderia automatica
library	la biblioteca
newspaper seller	il giornalaio
pharmacy	la farmacia
police station	il posto di polizia
post office	la posta
shoe store	il negozio di scarpe
souvenirs	il negozio di oggetti ricordo
sporting goods	il negozio di articoli sportivi
stationery store	la cartoleria
tobacco shop	la tabaccheria, il tabaccaio
toy shop	il negozio di giocattoli
travel agency	l'agenzia di viaggi

At the pharmacy

antibiotic	l'antibiotico
antiseptic cream	la crema antisettica
aspirins	le aspirine
bandage	la garza, la benda
Band-Aids	i cerotti
cotton wool	l'ovatta
cough lozenges	le pasticche per la tosse
eye drops	le gocce per gli occhi
laxative	il lassativo
medicine	la medicina
pills	le compresse
prescription	la ricetta
sleeping pills	i sonniferi
tablets	le pastiglie

Toiletries and other items

aftershave	la lozione dopobarba
baby food	gli alimenti per bebè
brush	la spazzola
comb	il pettine
contact-lens liquid	il liquido per lenti a contatto
contraceptives	gli anticoncezionali
cream	la crema
deodorant	il deodorante
disposable diapers	i pannolini
perfume	il profumo
razor	il rasoio
razor blades	la lamette
safety pins	le spille di sicurezza
sanitary napkins	gli assorbenti igienici
shampoo	lo shampoo
shaving cream	la crema da barba
soap	il sapone
sunglasses	gli occhiali da sole
suntan lotion	la crema solare
talc	il talco
tampons	i tamponi igienici
tissues	i fazzolettini di carta
toothbrush	lo spazzolino da denti
toothpaste	il dentifricio

VOCABULARY

Food

Fruit (la frutta)

apple	la mela
apricot	l'albicocca
banana	la banana
cherry	la ciliegia
grapes	l'uva
fig	il fico
lemon	il limone
lime	il cedro
melon	il melone
orange	l'arancia
peach	la pesca
pear	la pera
pineapple	l'ananas
plum	la susina
raspberries	i lamponi
strawberries	le fragole
walnuts	le noci
watermelon	l'anguria

Vegetables (la verdura)

artichoke	il carciofo
asparagus	gli asparagi
beans	i fagioli
cabbage	il cavolo
carrot	la carota
cauliflower	il cavolfiore
chicory	l'indivia
cucumber	il cetriolo
garlic	l'aglio
leek	il porro
lettuce	l'insalata
mushrooms	i funghi
olives	le olive
onion	la cipolla
parsley	il prezzemolo
peas	i piselli
pepper	il peperone
potato	la patata
spinach	gli spinaci
string beans	i fagiolini
tomato	il pomodoro
zucchini	gli zucchini

Meat (la carne) and poultry (il pollame)

beef	il manzo
kidneys	i rognoni
lamb	l'agnello
lamb cutlet	cotoletta d'agnello
liver	il fegato
pork	il maiale
pork chops	braciole di maiale
steak	la bistecca
veal	il vitello
veal cutlet	scaloppina di vitello
chicken	il pollo
chicken breasts	petti di pollo
duck	l'anatra

Fish (i pesci) and shellfish (frutti di mare)

anchovies	le acciughe
bass	il branzino
clams	le vongole
cod	il merluzzo
cuttlefish	la seppia
eel	l'anguilla
lobster	l'aragosta
mackerel	lo sgombro
mussels	le cozze
octopus	il polpo
oyster	l'ostrica
prawns	i gamberoni
red mullet	la triglia
salmon	il salmone
sardines	le sardine
squid	i calamari
trout	la trota
tuna	il tonno

Parts of the body (il corpo)

ankle	la caviglia
arm	il braccio
back	la schiena
blood	il sangue
bone	l'osso
chest	il torace
ear	l'orecchio
eye	l'occhio
face	il viso
finger	il dito
foot	il piede
hair	i capelli
hand	la mano
head	la testa
heart	il cuore
knee	il ginocchio
leg	la gamba
lung	il polmone
mouth	la bocca

VOCABULARY

muscle	il muscolo
nose	il naso
rib	la costola
shoulder	la spalla
skin	la pelle
stomach	lo stomaco
throat	la gola
toe	il dito del piede
tooth	il dente

Parts of the car (la macchina)

battery	la batteria
brakes	i freni
carburetor	il carburatore
clutch	la frizione
engine	il motore
exhaust pipe	il tubo di scappamento
fan belt	la cinghia del ventilatore
headlights	i fari
ignition	lo spinterogeno
plugs	le candele
tire	la gomma
turn signal	l'indicatore
wheel	la ruota
windshield	il parabrezza

Sports and games

athletics	l'atletica
basketball	la pallacanestro
chess	gli scacchi
climbing	l'alpinismo
cycling	il ciclismo
fishing	la pesca
golf	il golf
racing (car)	la corsa automobilistica
racing (horse)	la corsa di cavalli
sailing	la vela
skiing	lo sci
soccer	il calcio
swimming	il nuoto
tennis	il tennis
volleybal	la pallavolo

Sports equipment

I'd like to rent	Vorrei noleggiare . . .
bathing hut	una cabina
deck chair	una sedia a sdraio

fishing tackle	degli arnesi da pesca
game	il gioco
golf course	il campo da golf
match, game	la partita
pedal boat	un moscone
racket	una racchetta
rowboat	una barca a remi
sailboat	una barca a vela
skates	dei pattini
ski boots	degli scarponi da sci
ski poles	dei bastoncini
ski run	la pista
skis	degli sci
swimming pool	la piscina
tennis court	il campo da tennis
water skis	degli sci nautici
windsurfer	un surf, tavola a vela

Places to visit and natural features

art gallery	la galleria d'arte
bridge	il ponte
building	l'edificio
castle	il castello
cathedral	il duomo
chapel	la cappella
church	la chiesa
concert hall	la sala dei concerti
exhibit	la mostra
fountain	la fontana
gardens	i giardini
island	l'isola
lake	il lago
market	il mercato
monastery	il monastero
monument	il monumento
museum	il museo
palace	il palazzo
park	il parco
river	il fiume
ruins	le rovine
square	la piazza
stadium	lo stadio
statue	la statua
theater	il teatro
tower	la torre
town hall	il municipio
university	l'università

VOCABULARY

Italian–English Vocabulary

a at, in, to

abbastanza quite, rather

abitante *m.* inhabitant, resident

accanto a beside

accettare to accept

accomodarsi to make oneself comfortable; **s'accomodi** please do, go ahead, please sit down

accompagnare to accompany

accordo: d'accordo agreed, I agree

aceto *m.* vinegar

acqua *f.* water; **–minerale** mineral water

adesso now

aereo *m.* airplane

aeroporto *m.* airport

agenzia *(f.)* **di viaggi** travel agency

aggiungere to add

agnello *m.* lamb

agosto August

aiuto *m.* help

al, all', allo, alla, etc. at the, in the, to the

albergo *m.* hotel (plural **alberghi**)

alimentari *m. pl.* groceries

allora well then, now

alto/a tall, high; **–pressione** high pressure

altro/a other; **vuole altro?** do you want anything else? **senz'altro** of course

alzarsi to get up

ambasciata *f.* embassy

ambulanza *f.* ambulance

americano/a American

amica *(f.),* **amico** *(m.)* friend

anche too, also; **anch'io** me too

ancora yet

andata *f.* one-way (ticket); **–e ritorno** round-trip (ticket)

andare to go, drive; **andiamo** let's go; **– a letto** to go to bed

anello *m.* ring

anno *m.* year

antipasto *m.* appetizer (course)

aperto/a open

appartamento *m.* apartment

appuntamento *m.* appointment

apribottiglia *m.* bottle opener

aprile April

aprire to open

arancia *f.* orange

aria condizionata *f.* air-conditioning

arrivare to arrive

arriverderci, arrivederla goodbye

arrivo *m.* arrival

arrosto roasted

articolo *m.* article

ascensore *m.* elevator

ascoltare to listen to

aspettare to wait

assicurazione *f.* insurance

assortiti assorted

attenzione! careful!

attimo *m.* moment

attraversare to cross

augurare to wish

autonoleggio *m.* car rental

automobile *f.* car

automobilista *m./f.* motorist, driver

autostrada *f.* highway

autunno *m.* autumn

avere to have; **aver bisogno** to need

avvertire to warn

avvocato *m.* lawyer

azienda *f.* factory, firm; **–di soggiorno e turismo** tourist information office

bagaglio *m.* luggage

bagno *m.* bath, swim

balcone *m.* balcony

bambina *f.* girl

bambino *m.* child, boy

banca *f.* bank

bar *m.* bar, café

barbiere *m.* barber's

barca *f.* boat

basso/a low; **bassa pressione** low pressure

bastare to be enough; **basta!** enough! **basta così** that's all

bè . . . well

bel, bello/a lovely, beautiful, nice

bene fine, good well; **ben cotto/a** well-done (steak); **ben arrivato/a!** welcome! **va bene** fine, OK; **benissimo** excellent, great

benzina *f.* gas

bere to drink

bevanda *f.* (soft) drink, beverage

bianco/a white

bibita *f.* (soft) drink

bicchiere *m.* glass

bicicletta *f.* bicycle

biglietteria *f.* ticket window, counter

biglietto *m.* ticket; **–da visita** business card

VOCABULARY

binario *m.* track
birra *f.* beer
bisogno: aver– to need
bistecca *f.* steak
bitter *m.* type of aperitif
blu blue
bocca *f.* mouth
borsa *f.* handbag, purse
bottega *f.* workshop
bottiglia *f.* bottle
braccio *m.* arm
braciola *f.* chop; –di maiale pork chop
brindisi *m.* toast
brutto bad
buca *(f.)* delle lettere mailbox
buonanotte good night
buonasera good evening
buongiorno good morning
buono/a good
burro *m.* butter

cabina *(f.)* telefonica telephone booth
cadere to fall
cacciatore: alla– cooked in sauce
 containing onions, tomatoes,
 mushrooms, peppers, wine
caffè *m.* coffee, café
caffelatte *m.* coffee / with milk
calcio *m.* soccer
caldo hot
calmo calm
cambio *m.* exchange, rate of exchange
camera *f.* room, bedroom
cameriera *f.* waitress
cameriere *m.* waiter
camicia *f.* shirt
campanile *m.* bell tower
campeggio *m.* campsite, camping
campo *m.* field; –da tennis tennis court
capire to understand
cappello *m.* hat
carabinieri *m. pl.* police
caraffa *f.* jug, carafe
carne *f.* meat
caro/a expensive
carta *f.* paper; –di credito credit card;
 –stradale map; –verde green card
 (car insurance); –d'identità identity
 card
cartolina *f.* postcard
casa *f.* house, home
casereccio/a homemade (bread etc.)
caso *m.* case
cassa *f.* cashier

castello *m.* castle
cavallo *m.* horse; andare a–to ride
cena *f.* supper
cenare to have supper
centralinista *m./f.* telephone operator
centro *m.* center
ceramista *m.* potter
cercare to look for
cerotto *m.* Band-Aid
certo certainly
che? what?
chiamare to call; to telephone
chiamarsi to be called
chiave *f.* key
chiesa *f.* church
chilo *m.* kilo
chilometro *m.* kilometer
chiudere to close
chiuso/a closed
chiusura *f.* closing
ci here, there; c'è there is; ci sono there
 are
ciao! hello! goodbye!
cielo *m.* sky
cinema *m.* cinema
cintura *f.* belt
circa about
città *f.* town, city
cognome *m.* surname
coincidenza *f.* connection
colazione *f.* breakfast
colore *m.* color
coltello *m.* knife
come as, like, how; come? how? what?
cominciare to begin
comodo/a comfortable
compilare to fill out (form)
completo/a full
comprare to buy
compressa *f.* pill
compreso/a included
con with
concerto *m.* concert
conoscere to know (person or place)
consigliare to advise
conto *m.* bill, account
contorno *m.* vegetable (with main dish
 in restaurant)
controllare to check
controllo *(m.)* passaporti passport
 control
contusione *f.* bruise
coperto *m.* cover charge; overcast
 (sky)

corriera *f.* coach, bus
corso *m.* avenue
cosa *f.* thing; **che cosa? cosa?** what?
così like this, thus; **così così** so so
costare to cost
cotoletta *f.* cutlet; **—alla milanese** dipped in egg and breadcrumbs, then fried
cotone *m.* cotton
credo I think
crudo raw; **prosciutto—** smoked ham
cucchiaio *m.* spoon
cucina *f.* kitchen

da at, by, for, from, of
dal, dall', dallo, dalla, etc. at the, by the, for the, from the, of the
dare to give
davanti in front
davvero? really?
del, dell', dello, della, etc. of the, some, any
denaro *m.* money
dente *m.* tooth
dentista *m./f.* dentist
dentro inside
denuncia *f.* report (to the police)
desiderare to want; **desidera? desiderano?** what would you like?
dessert *m.* dessert, sweet
destinazione *f.* destination
destra *f.* right; **a—** to/on the right; **sulla—** on the right
deve (see **dovere**)
deviazione *f.* detour
dicembre December
dichiarare to declare
dietro behind
dimenticare, dimenticarsi to forget
dire to say, tell
diretto direct; *m.* train making many stops
direttore *m.* director, manager
direzione *f.* direction, management
diritto straight ahead
discoteca *f.* discotheque
disegnatrice *f.* designer
dispiace: mi— I'm sorry
disponibile available
ditta *f.* firm, company
divertirsi to enjoy oneself
doccia *f.* shower
documento *m.* document
dogana *f.* customs
dolce *m.* dessert, sweet

dollaro *m.* dollar
domanda *f.* question
domani tomorrow
domenica Sunday
domicilio *m.* place of residence
donna *f.* lady
dopo after
dopodomani the day after tomorrow
doppio/a double
dormire to sleep
dove? where? **dov'è?** where is?
dovere to have to; **deve prendere il treno** you must take the train
dritto straight ahead
dunque well, so
duomo *m.* cathedral

e and
è (see **essere**)
ecco here is
edificio *m.* building
elenco *(m.)* **telefonico** telephone directory
entrare to enter
entrata *f.* entrance
errore *m.* mistake
esame *m.* exam
esattamente exactly
esaurito sold out
espresso *m.* fast train
essere to be
est *m.* east
estate *f.* summer; **d'—** in the summer
estero: all'— abroad
etto *m.* 100 grams

facchino *m.* porter
famiglia *f.* family
fare to do, make; **—il biglietto** to buy one's ticket; **una settimana fa** a week ago
farmacia *f.* pharmacy
favoloso/a fabulous, great
favore: per— please
febbraio February
febbre *f.* fever, temperature
fegato *m.* liver
felice happy
fermarsi to stop
fermata *f.* bus stop
ferroviaria: la stazione— railroad station
fetta *f.* slice
fidanzata *f.* fiancée; **fidanzato** fiancé
figlia *f.* daughter
figlio *m.* son

VOCABULARY

fiammiferi *m. pl.* matches
fine *f.* end
finesettimana *m.* weekend
finestra *f.* window
finire to finish
fino a as far as, until
Firenze Florence
firma *f.* signature
firmare to sign
fondo: **in—** at/to the end, bottom, back
fontana *f.* fountain
forchetta *f.* fork
formaggio *m.* cheese
fornello *(m.)* **a gas** gas stove
forno *m.* oven; **al—** baked
forse perhaps
forte strong
fotografare to photograph
fragola *f.* strawberry
francese French
Francia France
francobollo *m.* stamp
fratello *m.* brother
freddo/a cold
frittata *f.* omelette
fritto/a fried: **—misto** dish of mixed fried fish
fronte: **di—** opposite; **di—a** in front of
frullato *m.* milkshake
frutta *f.* fruit; **frutti di mare** shellfish
fruttivendolo *m.* fruit store
fumatori *m. pl.* smokers
fungo *m.* mushroom; **i funghi** mushrooms
funzionare to work (of machines)
furto *m.* robbery
fuori outside

gabinetto *m.* toilet
galleria *f.* art gallery; box seat (theater)
Galles Wales
gallese Welsh
gamba *f.* leg
garage *m.* garage
gasolio *m.* diesel
gassato/a fizzy, carbonated
gelateria *f.* ice-cream parlor
gelato *m.* ice cream
gente *f.* people
genitore *m.* parent
gennaio January
gentile kind
gettone *m.* telephone token
ghiacciato/a frozen

ghiaccio *m.* ice
già already
giacca *f.* jacket
giallo/a yellow
giardino *m.* garden
giocare to play
gioco *m.* game, play
giornale *m.* newspaper
giornata *f.* day
giorno *m.* day
giovane *m.* young man
giovedì Thursday
girare to turn; **giri** turn
giro *m.* tour
gita *f.* trip
giugno June
gli the (m. pl.); to him
gola *f.* throat
gomma *f.* tire
gondola *f.* gondola
gonna *f.* skirt
grado *m.* degree
grammo *m.* gram
Gran Bretagna Great Britain
grande big
grave serious
grazie thank you; **—mille** many thanks
grigio/a gray
griglia: **alla—** grilled
guadagnare to earn
guardare to watch, look at
guasto *m.* breakdown
guidare to guide

ho, hai, ha, hanno (see **avere**)
hotel *m.* hotel

i the (m. pl.)
ieri yesterday
il the (m. sing.)
imparare to learn
importa: **non—** it doesn't matter
in in, to
incassare to cash
inchiesta *f.* survey
incidente *m.* accident
incominciare to begin
incrocio *m.* crossroads, corner
indigestione *f.* indigestion
indirizzo *m.* address
informazione *f.* information
Inghilterra England
inglese English
ingresso *m.* entrance

VOCABULARY

insalata *f.* salad
insegnante *m./f.* teacher
insegnare to teach
insieme together
isola *f.* island
Italia Italy
italiano/a Italian

la the (f. sing.); you, her, it
lago *m.* lake
lana *f.* wool
largo/a wide (plural larghi/e)
lasciare to leave
latte *m.* milk
latteria *f.* dairy
lavarsi to wash (oneself)
lavorare to work
lavoro *m.* work, job
le the (f. pl.); to/for you
lei you (sing.); she; her
lentamente slowly
lento/a slow
letto *m.* bed
li them
lì there; lì in fondo down there
libero/a free
libreria *f.* bookstore
lieto: molto— nice to meet you
limonata *f.* lemonade
limone *m.* lemon
linea *f.* line; resti in— hold the line
lingua *f.* language
lira *f.* lira (unit of currency)
litro *m.* liter
lo the (m. sing.); him, it
Londra London
lontano/a far
loro their
luglio July
lui he, him
lunedì Monday
lungo/a long (plural lunghi/e)

ma but
macchina *f.* car, machine; —fotografica camera
macellaio *m.*, macelleria *f.* butcher's
madre *f.* mother
maggio May
maggiore eldest, major
maglione *m.* sweater
magro/a lean (meat)
mai never
maiale *m.* pork

mal: —di testa headache; —di stomaco stomachache; —di denti toothache
malato/a ill, sick
male bad, badly; non c'è male not bad; fa— to hurt
mamma *f.* mommy
mancia *f.* tip
mandare to send
mangiare to eat
mano *f.* hand (plural le mani)
manzo *m.* beef
mare *m.* sea
marito *m.* husband
marrone brown
martedì Tuesday
marzo March
matrimoniale: camera— room with double bed
mattina *f.* morning
meccanico *m.* mechanic
medico *m.* doctor
meglio better
mela *f.* apple
meno less; —un quarto quarter to (time)
menù *m.* menu
mercato *m.* market
mercoledì Wednesday
mese *m.* month
messaggio *m.* message
metro *m.* meter
metropolitana *f.* subway
mettere to put
mezzanotte midnight
mezzo/a half; —pensione half-board; mezz'ora half an hour
mezzogiorno noon
mi me; to/for me; myself
migliore better
milanese: alla— dipped in egg and breadcrumbs and fried
mille thousand
minestra *f.* soup
mio, mia, etc. my, mine
misto/a mixed
moda *f.* fashion
modello *m.* model, type
moderno/a modern
modo *m.* way, manner
moglie *f.* wife
molto a lot (of), many; very (much)
mondo *m.* world
monte *m.* mountain
montagna *f.* mountain(s)
monumento *m.* monument

morire to die
mortadella *f.* type of sausage
mostra *f.* exhibit
mostrare to show
motocicletta *f.* motorcycle
mozzarella *f.* type of cheese
museo *m.* museum
musica *f.* music

nascere to be born
Natale Christmas
nazionalità *f.* nationality
ne some (of it/of them)
nebbia *f.* fog
negoziante *m.* shop owner
negozio *m.* shop
nel, nell', nello, nella, etc. in the
nero/a black
nessun, nessuno/a no, none; nobody
neve *f.* snow
niente nothing
no no
noleggiare to rent
noleggio *m.* rental, hire
nome *m.* name
non not
nonna *f.* grandmother
nord *m.* north; **nord-ovest** northwest
normale normal; regular (gas)
nostro/a our
notte *f.* night
novembre November
nulla anything, nothing
numero *m.* number; size (shoe); **—
   sbagliato** wrong number; **—di
   immatriculazione** registration
   number
nuotare to swim
nuoto *m.* swimming
nuovo/a new
nuvola *f.* cloud
nuvoloso cloudy

o or
occhiali *m. pl.* glasses; **—da sole**
   sunglasses
occupato/a occupied
offerta *f.* offer
oggi today
ogni every
olio *m.* oil
oliva *f.* olive
ombra *f.* shade
ombrellone *m.* beach umbrella

opera *f.* opera, work
oppure or else
ora *f.* time, hour; **—di pranzo** lunchtime
orario *m.* timetable; **—di visita** opening
   hours
orecchio *m.* ear
orologio *m.* clock, watch
ospedale *m.* hospital
ostello *(m.)* **della gioventù** youth hostel
ottimo/a excellent, great
ottobre October
ovest west

pacchetto *m.* pack
padre *m.* father
paese *m.* village, country
pagare to pay
paio *m.* pair
palazzo *m.* palace
pane *m.* bread
panetteria *f.* bakery
panino *m.* roll (bread)
panna *f.* cream
pantaloni *m. pl.* pants
parcheggiare to park
parcheggio *m.* parking, parking lot
parlare to speak
parrucchiere *m.* hair stylist
parte *f.* part; **a—** separately
partenza *f.* departure
partire to depart, leave
partita *(f.)* **di calcio** soccer game
pasaggio: di— en route, on the way
passante *m.* passerby
passaporto *m.* passport
passare to spend, pass; **—per** to go
   along
passo *m.* step; **a due passi** very close
   (two steps)
pasticceria *f.* bakery (with cakes)
pasto *m.* meal
patata *f.* potato
patente *f.* driver's license
pattini *m. pl.* skates; **—a rotelle** roller
   skates
peccato: che peccato! what a pity!
pecorino *m.* sheep's milk cheese
pedaggio *m.* toll charge
peggio worse
pelle *f.* leather
pellicola *f.* film (roll)
penna *f.* pen
pensione *(f.)* **completa** full board
pepe *m.* pepper

VOCABULARY

per for
pera *f*. pear
perchè because, why?
perdere to lose
pericoloso dangerous
permesso allowed
pescare to fish
pesce *m*. fish
pescheria *f*. seafood store
piacere to please; **mi piace** I like (it); **mi piaccio no** I like (them)
piacere *m*. pleasure; pleased to meet you; **per—** please
piano *m*. floor, story; **pianterreno** ground floor, first floor
pianta *f*. town map
piatto *m*. plate, dish
piazza *f*. square
piccante strong (flavored)
piccolo/a small
piede *m*. foot; **a piedi** on foot, walking
pieno/a full; **fare il pieno** to fill up (with gas)
pila *f*. battery
pioggia *f*. rain
piombo *m*. lead
piovere to rain
piscina *f*. swimming pool
più more, most; **più che** more than; **di più** most of all; **in più** over and above **non . . . più** not anymore, no longer
po': **un po'di** a little (bit) of
poco: **un poco** a little
poi then
polizia *f*. police
pollo *m*. chicken
poltrone *f. pl.* box seats (theater)
pomeriggio *m*. afternoon
pomodoro *m*. tomato
ponte *m*. bridge
portabagagli *m*. trunk (of car); porter
portafoglio *m*. wallet
portare to bring, carry, take
possibile possible
posso I can (see **potere**)
posta *f*. post office
posto *m*. seat; job
potere to be able
pranzare to have lunch
pranzo *m*. lunch
preferire to prefer
prefisso *m*. area code
prego not at all, don't mention it

prego? what would you like?
prelevare to withdraw (cash)
prendere to take; to catch (train, etc.); to have (drink, etc.)
prenotare to reserve, book
prenotazione *f*. reservation, booking
preoccuparsi to be worried
prescrivere to prescribe
presentare to present
pressione *f*. pressure
presto early, soon
preventivo *m*. estimate
previsioni del tempo weather forecast
previsto/a expected
prezzo *m*. price
primavera *f*. spring
primo/a first; **per primo** as a first course; **la prima colazione** breakfast
profumo *m*. perfume
pronto ready; hello! (on telephone); **— soccorso** first aid
proprio really, just; **—qui** just here
prosciutto *m*. ham
prossimo/a next
provare to try, to try on
provenienza *f*. origin, starting from
pullman *m*. coach
punto/a stung (from **pungere** to sting)
puntura *f*. sting; **—d'insetto** insect bite
pure: entri— come in, of course

quadro *m*. painting, picture
qualcosa something
quando? when?
quanto? how much?; **quant'è?** how much is it? **quanti/e?** how many?
quarto *m*. quarter
quel, quell', quello, quella that; **quei, quegli, quelle** those
questo/a this; **questi/e** these
qui here

raffreddore *m*. cold
ragazza *f*. girl; **ragazzo** *m*. boy
rallentare to slow down
rapido *m*. fast intercity express train
respirare to breathe
retro: vista sul— gives onto the back (of building)
ricetta *f*. prescription
ricevimento *m*. reception
ricevuto *f*. receipt
ricordarsi to remember
riduzione *f*. reduction

rimanere to stay, remain
rimettere to pull back
riparare to repair
riscaldamento *m.* heating
riservare to reserve
ristorante *m.* restaurant
ritardo *m.* delay; **in—** late
ritornare to return
ritorno: andata e— round-trip ticket
riuscire to succeed
rivista *f.* magazine
rosso/a red
roulotte *f.* trailer
rovescio *m.* shower (of rain)
rubare to steal; **mi è stato rubato . . .**
   my . . . has been stolen

sabato Saturday
sacchetto *m.* bag
sala *f.* room; **—da pranzo** dining room
salame *m.* salami sausage
sale *m.* salt
salumeria *f.* delicatessen, grocery store
salsa *f.* sauce
saltimbocca alla romana dish
   consisting of slices of ham and veal
   fried in butter then braised in white
   wine
sandali *m. pl.* sandals
sangue: al— rare (steak)
sapere to know
sbagliare to make a mistake
sbagliato mistaken, wrong
scacchi *m. pl.* chess
scarpe *f. pl.* shoes
scatola *f.* box, tin
scheda *f.* form
scegliere to choose
scendere to get off (bus, etc.)
sci *m.* skiing
sciare to ski
scontrino *m.* receipt
scorso/a last; **la settimana—** last week
Scozia *f.* Scotland
scozzese Scottish
scuola *f.* school
scusi! excuse me! I beg your pardon!
se if
secolo *m.* century
secondo/a second; **di—** for second
   course
sedia *f.* seat, chair
selvaggio/a wild
semaforo *m.* traffic lights

sempre always
senso unico one-way street
senta! senti! listen!
sentirsi to feel
senza without; **senz'altro** of course
sera *f.* evening
servire to serve
servizio *m.* service
seta *f.* silk
settembre September
settimana *f.* week
si one, you; yourself, oneself, himself,
   herself, themselves
sì yes
sicuro/a sure
sigaretta *f.* cigarette
signora *f.* lady, Mrs.
signor(e) *m.* gentleman, Mr.
signorina *f.* young lady, Miss
singolo/a single
sinistra *f.* left; **a—** to/on the left; **sulla—** on
   the left
so I know (see **sapere**); **non lo so** I don't
   know
soggiorno *m.* living room
soldi *m. pl.* money
sole *m.* sun
solo only, alone
soltanto only
sono I am; they are (see **essere**); **ci sono**
   there are
sorella *f.* sister
spazioso/a spacious, large
sperare to hope
spesa *f.* shopping
spesso often
spettacolo *m.* performance
spiaggia *f.* beach
spiccioli *m. pl* small change
spilla *f.* brooch
spingere to push
sport *m.* sport
sposarsi to get married
sposato/a married
spremuta *f.* fresh fruit juice
stagione *f.* season
stamattina this morning
stanco/a tired
stanza *f.* room
stare to be (well, etc.); **come sta?** how
   are you?
stasera this evening
Stati Uniti United States
stato/a been (past part. of **essere**)
stazione *f.* station; **—ferroviaria** railroad

VOCABULARY

station; **—di servizio** service station
sterlina *f.* pound sterling
stesso/a same; **lo—** the same (thing)
strada *f.* street
stradale (of the) street
stravagante odd, strange
stretto/a narrow, tight
studente *m.* student
studiare to study
su on, up
subito at once, right away
succo *m.* juice
sud *m.* south
sugo *m.* sauce
sul, sull', sullo, sulla, etc. on the
suo, sua, etc. your, his, her, its
super premium (gas)
supermercato *m.* supermarket
supplemento *m.* surcharge
surf *m.* windsurfer, surfboard
surriscaldare to overheat

tabaccheria *f.* tobacco shop
tabaccaio *m.* tobacconist
taglia *f.* size (clothes)
taglio *m.* cutting
tanto/a so much, very much, a lot
tardi late
tariffa *f.* fare
tassì *m.* taxi
tavola *(f.)*/**tavolo** *(m.)* table
tazza *f.* cup
te you
tè *m.* tea
teatro *m.* theater
tedesco/a German
telefonata *f.* telephone call
tempo *m.* time, weather
temporale *m.* thunderstorm
tenda *f.* tent
tenero/a tender
terrazza *f.* terrace
testa *f.* head
ti you; to/for you
tirare to pull
toilette *f.* toilet
torace *m.* chest
tornare to return
torta *f.* cake
tosse *f.* cough
tovagliolo *m.* table napkin
traghetto *m.* ferry
trattoria *f.* restaurant
treno *m.* train

troppo too (much)
trovare to find
trovarsi to be (situated)
tu you (sing.)
tuo, tua, etc. your, yours
turismo *m.* tourism
turista *m./f.* tourist
tutto all, everything; **—a posto**
everything in order; **tutto/a** every, all
tutti e due both

ufficio *m.* office
ultimo/a last
un, un', uno, una a, an, one
università *f.* university
uomo *m.* man
uovo *m.* egg (plural *f.* **uova**)
usare to use
uscire to go out
uscita *f.* exit
uva *f.* grape(s)

va (see **andare**); **va bene** OK, fine
vacanza *f.* vacation
vada! go!
vado I'm going (see **andare**)
valigia *f.* suitcase
vaniglia *f.* vanilla
vaporetto *m.* motorboat
vecchio/a old
vedere to see
vedova *f.* widow
vela: far— to sail
veloce fast
vendere to sell
venerdì Friday
venire to come
vento *m.* wind
verde green
verdura *f.* vegetable
vermut *m.* vermouth
vero? isn't it? aren't you? etc.
verso about
vestito *m.* dress
vetrina *f.* store window
vettura *(f.)* **ristorante** dining car
vi to/for you; yourselves; there
via *f.* street
viaggiare to travel
viaggio *m.* trip, journey
viale *m.* avenue
vicino/a near
vietato/a prohibited
villetta *f.* small house

VOCABULARY

vino *m.* wine
visitare to visit
vista *f.* view
vita *f.* life
vitello *m.* veal
voi you (plural)
volere to want
volo *m.* flight
volta *f.* time; **qualche volta** sometimes

vomitare to be sick, vomit
vorrei I'd like (see **volere**)
vostro/a your
vuole (see **volere**)

zoccoli *m. pl.* clogs
zucchero *m.* sugar
zucchini *m. pl.* zucchini
zuppa *f.* soup